Comments from Public Sector Employees

"This book is great nourishment for those in charge of, or interested in, the care and feeding of a successful organization." - Chris Gonaver

"Over the years I have worked with Wendi, I have seen firsthand her ability to get positive results through improved customer service. Using a very common sense approach, this book provides excellent building blocks that readers can use to improve customer service in their own organizations." - Richard Haas Jr.

"Wendi Brick helped me see that I interacted with customers all day long - external customers coming in to do business as well as internal customers, and my fellow employees who needed information or assistance from me. The lessons I learned and the tools I received from her continue to help me on a day-to-day basis." - Holly Simonette

"In her book, "The Science of Service," Wendi Brick shows her readers how to improve customer service in their organizations in tangible, measurable ways. Even more importantly, she also makes a compelling case for why public agencies should make the effort." - Janice Graham Heather

The Science of Service

Six Essential Elements for Creating a Culture of Service

In the Public Sector

Wendi Pomerance Brick, MS

The Science of Service
Six Essential Elements for
Creating a Culture of Service In the Public Sector
Written by Wendi Pomerance Brick

Layout by CoCo Publishing
www.cocoassociates.com/publishing

Cataloging-in-Publication Data is on file with the Library of Congress
ISBN: 978-0-9831233-1-6

PRINTED IN THE UNITED STATES OF AMERICA
First Edition: November 2010

SPECIAL SALES
Books are available at special discounts for bulk purchases.
For more information, write to:

Customer Service Advantage, Inc.
555 Country Club Lane, Suite C-350
Escondido, CA 92026
info@thecsaedge.com
http://www.theCSAedge.com

CONTENTS

Acknowledgements

Before we get started, I'd like to thank you very much for reading this book. I appreciate your support and interest.

I've shared this journey with many people, and could never have gotten to the point of writing this book without every single one of them.

First and foremost, to my husband Don, and my parents, family and friends: you are my core and my foundation. Thank you for the strength and guidance you give so freely.

Second, to everyone who shaped my professional career and my personal life: you have influenced me in a way that is priceless, and have all taught me so much. Thank you for your rich contributions.

And finally, a wholehearted "thank you!" to the *jerk* in my first story. We might not be holding this book without you.

The Science of Service

Preface
A Public Servant is Born

I didn't grow up daydreaming about being a government employee. Did you? I ask that question all the time; almost no one says yes. Personally, I wanted to be a killer whale trainer at SeaWorld but life took me down a different road. And I'm so glad it did!

Years ago, during my last semester of (undergraduate) college, one of my professors sat me down for a chat. There was an intern position available with the county government of San Diego and she thought it would be a good fit for me. "I know the people who work there; they're really great. And I think you'll find the work interesting."

With a shrug and a smile, I gladly accepted her offer to write a recommendation for me. Then, I went out and bought my first suit.

A few weeks later, working away as an intern, I realized my professor was right. These people were great.

I found myself surrounded by people who came to work every day to improve other people's quality of life. From food inspectors to directors of public health programs for children to air and water safety managers – these people had dedicated their careers to helping our communities in ways that, if done correctly, would go completely unnoticed. I was really moved by that.

That summer internship opened my eyes to a whole new "big picture." By the time I started graduate school in the fall, I had a completely different career goal than I did just a few short months before. I had embraced the County's motto, "The Noblest Motive is the Public Good," as my own.

Trained on The Front Line

My first nine years of government work were spent as a Hazardous Materials Specialist and then an Environmental Health Specialist with the County of San Diego. I served as a public liaison for customer concerns and complaints. Part of my job was to "translate" technical information such as a Health Risk Assessment's cancer data into terms that a) people relate to, and b) would not cause an irate reaction. I was also involved in several projects that included facilitating contentious public meetings.

This information is relevant for one reason only: The tips and techniques in this book are far more than academic concepts; they are grounded in real-life, front-line experiences with customers – cranky customers. I assure you, these ideas have been tested and proven many times over.

The County recognized my efforts and results with our "customers," and when the first countywide customer service program was launched in 1998, I was hired as the Customer Service Manager.

Because the job had not previously existed, I asked, "What would you like me to do on my first day?"

The response was, "You have to figure that out." Oh. Then my new boss smiled and said, "Be a star, Wendi."

The Jerk Who Changed My Life

Soon after I started that job, I traveled to a five-day conference in San Francisco for customer service professionals from around the world. I took so many pages of notes that my head was spinning but I was so excited to hear keynote speeches from visionary leaders like Mrs. Fields, Tom Peters and Stephen Covey.

The Science of Service

As I made my way through the conference, I noticed something interesting: I couldn't find anyone else who worked in the government sector. Everyone I spoke to represented a private company. Looking through the list of attendees, I noticed a few government representatives – but there were over 1,500 people at the conference! Where were all the public employees?

Over lunch that day, it all became clear.

I was sitting with a group of eight people, all strangers to each other, and we took turns introducing ourselves. Feeling proud to represent the fine work of government employees, I was looking forward to my turn. When the time came, I sat up straight and said, "Hi. I'm Wendi and I'm the Customer Service Manager for the County of San Diego."

The man sitting next to me snorted and smirked, saying, "Customer service in government? Isn't that an oxymoron?"

Everyone at the table had a good laugh; I gulped, trying hard not to look angry. I looked down and held my tongue but underneath my carefully controlled exterior, I was burning with retorts that would make any New Yorker blush. Who was he to talk so condescendingly about the hardworking, dedicated employees I had come to respect and admire? I was proud of my choice to serve my community, and the caliber of dedication, intelligence and hard work I saw from my peers. I was insulted.

Looking back, I was probably a bit naïve. We have all heard people say:
- ▶ "government slackers"
- ▶ "they can't get a real job"
- ▶ "not smart enough to work in private industry"

The bad reputation of government workers has even worked its way into the English language. Think about the word "bureaucrat." Is it a positive or negative word? Once upon a time, not too long ago, it was a neutral noun for a person who worked in a government infrastructure. Today, common definitions include:

- ▶ An official who works by fixed routine without exercising intelligent judgment (Dictionary.com)
- ▶ Someone who works in or controls a bureaucracy. The term is often used negatively to describe a petty, narrow-minded person. (*American Heritage New Dictionary of Cultural Literacy*)
- ▶ An official in a bureaucracy, especially one who follows a routine in a mechanical, unimaginative way, insisting on proper forms, petty rules, etc. (*Webster's New World Dictionary*)

Public servants today work under the shadow of a very old reputation for bad service – even the ones hired yesterday. That's a lot to overcome before you even say hello to your first customer.

> *Whether or not we come across like narrow-minded bureaucrats is largely up to us.*

The truth is: we do work within a bureaucracy – that is, an organizational structure with procedures, protocols, and regulations to manage activity in large organizations – but whether or not we come across like narrow-minded bureaucrats is largely up to us.

As much of a jerk as that man was, I'm so thankful for his comment because he opened my eyes to a purpose. That day, I vowed to do everything I could, one person at a time, to change this poor perception of government employees. It became my mission to prove that truly extraordinary customer service could be the vehicle for that change.

Figuring it Out

Within two weeks of becoming the first Customer Service Manager, I was asked to submit an action plan including tasks and timelines for accomplishments over the next 12 months. I would be evaluated at the end of this 12-month period based on how well I achieved the goals I set.

My first thought was, "Ok Wendi, sink or swim. You wanted this. Start swimming."

It seemed like a good bit of research was in order so I set out to figure out who was known for great customer service – and why. Off to the bookstore I went (this was B.G. – before Google).

I spent many hours pouring through books about the finest service known to private business (because there weren't any on customer service in government). Also tremendously helpful were several studies that originated from then-Vice President Al Gore's movement to reinvent government.

After a couple of weeks of simmering all of the concepts down to the common denominators, the formula for great customer service (the Six Essential Elements) became crystal clear to me.

In the following chapters, I will be sharing the highlights of this research and the lessons that almost 20 years in government have taught me.

Fundamental Philosophy

In the wise words of Archimedes, "If you give me a lever and a place to stand, I can move the world." I have my place to stand: I believe in the value of public service, and that great customer service leaves an impression.

Until recently, I thought the lever had to be the backing of strong executive sponsorship – the kind of sponsorship where the sponsor not only believes in your project but gives you full support in making things happen. It's great if you have it; and make no mistake, it does make life easier. But I don't believe it's mission-critical anymore. In fact, I know it's not. The lever is YOU. You are both the belief and the action. If you make the decision, you make it happen.

> *Everyone has a sphere of influence. You don't have to be a manager to be a leader. Management is a title. Leadership is a choice.*

Everyone has a sphere of influence. You don't have to be a manager to be a leader. Management is a title. Leadership is a choice.

The decision to make a great impression on every person, every day, is entirely up to you. Understand that every time you answer the phone, you are the whole organization to that customer. The impression you leave will become a lasting impression of the entire organization and of government in general. All of these impressions, of all the people in the community, become the reputation of the organization.

That's means you have a huge responsibility. Fortunately, it's also a huge opportunity.

Thank you for being a champion of great service in government. It's not an easy role. As a public servant, you will come up against some very daunting obstacles including but not limited to: difficult customers, poor public perception, negative media stories, complicated politics, lack of budget and resources, uncooperative coworkers and bosses who may not share your vision.

Do what you can. Every person, every day, every contact makes a difference. Change what you can and you will certainly leave the world a better place.

Chapter One

Service in the Public Sector: Who Are the Customers and What Do They Want?

Define Customer – As Everyone

When the "customer service in government" movement started in the late 1990s, we spent a lot of time convincing government workers they even *had* customers*.

Those people who come into the lobby every day and ask for things? Oh, they aren't customers. They have to come here. We're the government.

The prevailing mindset was: "A government office isn't a business and the people we serve aren't customers."

With all due respect, I have to disagree. Progress requires that we take a broader view of the word *customer*, because in reality, **anyone you serve is a customer** – and we serve a lot of people in our everyday interactions: our co-workers, vendors, program beneficiaries and more.

In that light, and in the true spirit of service, customers are: **Every Person, Every Day.**

Every person you come into contact with is forming an impression of you, and by extension, your organization. Every person, every day. That includes a lot more people than you might think.

There are "external customers" – anyone outside of the organization such as a service recipient, citizen of your

---

* While the concepts shared in this book are specifically focused on public organizations such as local, regional, state and federal entities, they can also be applied to other large organizations such as school districts, nonprofits, healthcare organizations and others.

jurisdiction, business owner, child needing healthcare, tourist, a representative from another agency, an immigrant or a journalist.

We also have "internal customers" – people we interact with by phone, computer or in person in order to get the job done. For most government employees, there are a lot of internal customers: co-workers, colleagues, employees, bosses and other departments that rely on you.

Regardless of where a customer comes from, providing great service WILL pay off.

Every single person you encounter in your workday is forming an impression of you, your work, your supervisor, your department and your organization – every single time they interact with you. From internal to external customers, there are a lot of people noticing the service you provide and forming opinions about it.

Do you want to be trusted by others and held in high esteem? Or be seen as a mindless cog in the wheels of government? It's YOUR reputation. Invest in it.

Speaking of Reputations...

The reputation of your organization directly impacts your day-to-day life on the job. It's a no-brainer – if people have a good opinion of you and how you work, they are going to have a relaxed and friendly attitude about working with you.

Unfortunately, *people expect to have problems* when they work with government agencies. They expect to have trouble finding the answers to their questions. They expect long waits, and expect to encounter government employees who don't seem to care about them. If you were a customer calling for assistance, and you believed you would be treated rudely, kept on hold forever, get the run around and waste a lot of time – what is your attitude going to be when the service rep answers the phone?

Customers who walk into your office believing they will receive poor service are harder to assist. Their attitude toward you will be armored at best, combative at worst. If they have already formed a bad impression of your office before you even have a chance to assist them, you are fighting an uphill battle from the start.

Unfortunately, many of us are doing just that.

Why It's So Hard to Deliver Excellent Customer Service From a Government Desk

You come to work every day wanting to do a good job. Most of us really do want to help all the people who call, e-mail and walk in. Under ideal circumstances, you would have smooth, easy interactions with everyone you encounter during the workday: those within the organization, clients, vendors, visitors, media people, elected officials, special interest groups and the ordinary citizens served by the department.

You want to do a good job, and you are trying, but as it turns out – you work in a minefield. Unseen hazards could blow up at any moment! In fact, the next explosion may be just a phone call away.

Challenging Fact #1:
Some of your customers won't like you. Be nice anyway.

As often happens in government relations, by the time you pick up the phone, your caller is already upset. Why do people get so mad? It's a good question to ask because it helps you see things through customers' eyes.

As it turns out, there are a lot of reasons the caller could be angry – and more often than not, there are *valid* reasons. Let's explore a few from the customer's perspective.

Government customers do not *want* to interact with you; they *must* interact with you. If they wish to accomplish a task, they have no choice but to work with you. Probably 99 percent of the time, they would rather be doing something else.

Interacting with the government is stressful, and often done only under duress. Think of a police officer with the lights flashing in your rear-view mirror. Many interactions with public employees are definitely not optional!

Public processes tend to be cumbersome. In a world where immediate gratification is highly valued, the government can seem like an archaic behemoth. As we know all too well, in government, there is no shortage of rules, regulations, fees, codes, policies or procedures. Because you represent the department, YOU seem cumbersome – no matter how efficiently you serve your customer. (Not fair but true nonetheless.)

Government employees often have to say no and enforce rules. If this is your role, you can't expect to be popular.

Government processes can be expensive. Governments require certain permits, licenses, reviews and sign-offs, and those services often cost the customer both time and money.

Challenging Fact #2:
In government, customer satisfaction is NOT guaranteed.

Great customer service is harder to provide and sustain in government than it is in private industry. Perhaps more importantly, customer service in government is not defined the same way as it is in private industry.

Unlike the customer-centric culture of a corporation, we are not driven by brand capital and market share. Public sector employees must focus on high-quality service delivery not necessarily the customer's satisfaction with the final answer. Here's why:

Our customers are not "always right." We are often required to enforce laws and regulations designed to protect the public health, safety and environment. People who violate the regulations are guilty of a crime. The enforcer won't say, "You've clearly broken the law here but we want you to come back and see us again soon so don't worry about it. Have a nice day!"

The Science of Service

For many public services, we are not aiming for repeat customers. Think drunk drivers and polluters: the fewer the better. Another good example is public assistance – we want to help people become self-sufficient not to remain on aid programs long-term.

Quite often, our customers are captive. For many services, there's just nowhere else to go. If you want to buy a shirt and you aren't treated well in store number one, you can walk into store number two. But if you want a building permit and you aren't treated well, tough luck! This captive relationship is stressful for the customer. Without that competitive motivation to perform well, customers sometimes view government employees as unmotivated, detached or arrogant – before we even say hello.

(There are obvious exceptions to this. Many government services do compete with private enterprises such as a county-run animal shelter competing with the Humane Society or a private shelter, and parks and recreation facilities. These programs benefit greatly from repeat customers.)

Challenging Fact #3:
Bad service is quite memorable – and usually discussed.

We have all had experiences with bad service. In fact, if I asked you now, I'm sure you could easily recall a story about bad service that you once endured. Bad service stories are so easy to remember.

The interesting thing is: it's much harder to remember great service.

(No one remembers average service. Has anyone ever said to you "Hey, I ate at this highly-mediocre restaurant for lunch today. The food was OK; the service was average and the atmosphere – forgettable." Probably not. Stories of mediocre service usually go untold, and that's probably for the best. They aren't very riveting.)

The most significant thing to remember about bad service is that people talk about it – *a lot more than they talk about great service.* If your customers get bad service from your department, you can be sure they will be vocal about it. On average, we tell five times more people about bad service than great service. Moreover, when we vent on the Internet (think YouTube, Merchant Circle, Yelp and Kudzu), our bad reviews reach thousands of people.

Every person who speaks – positively or negatively – about the service you provide becomes a spokesperson for your entire organization.

Putting that in a larger context, every person who speaks – positively or negatively – about the service you provide becomes a spokesperson for your entire organization. It pays to get invested in the kind of message they broadcast.

In our line of work, a negative report about an organization can be catastrophic especially if those opinions are picked up by the media and broadcast to hundreds of thousands of people. These comments can affect programs, funding, staffing, service levels and most definitely political support.

If people in the community are voicing concerns about the quality of the service delivered at your organization's front counters, how long do you think it will be before you hear about it from the elected officials?

Every time you pick up the phone, send an e-mail or greet someone walking through the door, you represent your entire organization. To that person, you are "the City of…" or "the County of…" or "the XYZ Water District." That is a very powerful position because it gives you the power to influence public perception. Whatever impression you make on that person, they will extend to your entire organization. Those impressions, passed along through word-of-mouth at social

The Science of Service

events and business meetings, become the foundation of your organization's reputation.

Wouldn't you rather work at an organization that has a great reputation in the community? When I introduce myself as a government employee, I want people to say, "Really? Wow! I've heard SO many great things about your agency. When my grandmother called your office a year ago, the people there were so nice and helpful to her. I'd love to work in a place like that. Are there any openings?" It sure would be nicer than a lot of comments we get.

Influence public perception. Whatever impression you make on that person, they will extend to your entire organization.

Let's take a closer look at the details that our customers are most likely to notice – and discuss – about our service.

Universal Signs of Bad Service

▶ No greeting or acknowledgement

▶ Lack of eye contact

▶ "Less-than-friendly" body language or facial expressions

▶ Employees "missing in action" – not enough staff available to assist

▶ Ineffective communication among staff, departments or programs

▶ Information is difficult to find

▶ Staff are unwilling or unable to help

▶ Inconsistent answers among staff

▶ Getting the runaround

▶ Attitude of not caring

▶ Long lines

This isn't rocket science; we all know what bad service looks like. And how frustrating it can be for the customer – and how quickly a reputation for poor service can spread.

And sometimes, we even know we're giving it.

So let's get honest and ask the tough question: Why do we let bad service happen?

Perhaps we're just a bunch of mean, rotten people who truly stink at our jobs. Or, it could be that staff members wake up in the morning and think to themselves, "I can't wait to go to work today and provide really bad service. I mean horrible. The worst!"

While you may know someone you *suspect* of having these feelings (don't we all), in general this is certainly not the case. The vast majority of civil servants believe in the programs and services they serve. Most of us go to work every day to make our communities a better place to live. We understand how important our work is to the public, and many of us are quite passionate about the contribution we make.

Now, that said, I'm not as naïve as I used to be. I was a government employee for 18 years, and I have known thousands upon thousands of government workers. I've seen the slackers here and there, people who only come in to collect a paycheck but the vast majority of government workers are committed, hard-working employees.

So, if we rarely *intend* to provide poor service… why is our service perceived so poorly?

What Do *They* Want?

It can be difficult to get personally invested in delivering great service – especially if you don't like many of your (difficult) customers or you become defensive after being attacked for a while. A natural reaction is to form an "us vs. them" attitude in relation to your customers.

The Science of Service

In seminars and workshops for public servants, participants usually relate to customers as "them." *They* are so demanding. *They* are ignorant of the rules. *They* ask me the same questions over and over again. *They* keep me so busy I don't have time to do my real work. *They* lie.

Some government workers really have a negative attitude about the people they serve. Why does that happen?

In my experience, many civil servants got into government to perform a specific role (firefighter) or work in a specific field (criminal forensics) or support a specific cause (protect the environment). Some "just ended up" in government but really came to appreciate the important work that everyone does every day to protect the environment, public safety and more. All in all, we tend to be a committed and inspired group.

Unfortunately, many of us operate under very challenging conditions. With so many rules and regulations and difficult customers, it's enough to wear anyone down.

But, in all the agencies I've worked with, I have yet to see a formal program to support the workers in staying fresh, upbeat and engaged. So, naturally over time, many public employees become jaded and worn down. It's no wonder we lose touch with what "they" really want.

> *Over time, many public employees become jaded and worn down.*

What Would *You* Want?

The easiest way to see what "they" want is to close the gap. "They" is "us"… and we all want the same basic things.

I invite you to step into the shoes of a government customer, outside your own agency and outside of your comfort zone. See what it feels like to be on the other side of the desk. I did, and it was surprisingly eye-opening.

In 2009, I shared a traumatic experience with 10-15 percent of the American population: I was unexpectedly laid off. I applied for unemployment benefits. Unfortunately, I hit several snags in that process. When the expected check failed to arrive, I called the 800 number.

Two things happened, each of the eight times I called (yes, *eight times*):

I was forced to listen to a phone tree that was almost three minutes long.

After following instructions and pressing several numbers, I heard a message that said, "Due to a large volume of callers, no one is available to take your call. Goodbye."

By this time, three weeks had gone by with no contact and my blood pressure was rising. All I wanted was to talk to someone!

I finally found a website and sent an e-mail to the noted contact. Soon I received a call in response but as luck would have it, I was not home to answer it. The caller did not identify her name or the agency, and she left the original 800 number as the way to reach her. This pointless exchange happened three separate times before I finally requested a time-certain phone appointment. To my relief, this request was granted.

Can you imagine how exasperated I was when eight weeks later, I finally spoke to a live service rep? Nonetheless, he was professional and helpful, and we straightened out the situation.

More than ever before, I had a really clear view from *both* sides of the "customer service in government" table.

There's no doubt about it: when you work in government services, the customers can be impatient and demanding. It goes with the territory, as they say. So, if you work with the public, a patient and understanding mindset is absolutely critical.

It helps to remember that most of your customers are under a LOT of pressure – time or financial constraints, significant health issues, severe family crises and many other stressors. If the tables were turned, you would be demanding, too. A little patience and understanding go a long way with agitated people.

> *A little patience and understanding go a long way with agitated people.*

The bottom line is this: a public servant's job is to serve. You come to work every day for the unique opportunity to make people's lives better, help them solve their problems or protect them from harm. If the people you serve are demanding or frustrated or angry, it has nothing to do with *you*. They are angry or frustrated with their *situation* – and they are in dire need of assistance.

If you can control your reactions and not get defensive or take things personally, you can make a positive difference for people. In fact, you can do such a good job solving their problems that they actually thank you at the end of the call.

Universal Customer Desires

As it turns out, all customers want the same four basic things, every single time:

- ▶ To be treated with dignity and respect
- ▶ To have some control
- ▶ To be understood
- ▶ Resolution of the issue

Let's take a closer look at each one.

1. Respect

All people want is to be treated with dignity and respect. These two elements add grease to the wheels of any interaction, easing relations and facilitating progress. With respect, everyone moves forward. When it's missing, progress is hampered.

Do you see your customer as the reason for your work or an interruption to your day? When the phone starts ringing, do you ever want to roll your eyes?

It's ok if you do. It's a common reaction, really. We're all busy running around all day, not twiddling our thumbs waiting for something to do. (I know, there are some people who appear to be doing nothing a lot of the time. We're not talking about them, we're talking about you. And you're busy, right?)

Let's be fair: it's not really that you think the customer should be ignored. It may be that you think his or her issue is just not as important as the one you are tending to.

The first step in respecting someone is to see him or her as fundamentally valuable and important. That may seem obvious but in government work, it's not always easy. Let's say your boss announces that by tomorrow morning, he wants you to review your budget and suggest ways to meet a five percent cut. Then your phone rings; it could be an internal or external customer. Regardless, whatever they want to discuss with you may not seem as important to you in that moment as it is to them. It can be difficult to refocus your attention on the customer and respect his or her needs.

In a workshop that I facilitated a few years ago for people who administer food stamps and welfare, we were discussing the components of great service including promptness. As I explained that, "Good service is fast service," I noticed a woman with a puzzled look on her face. She was so intent that I commented, "You look like you are really giving this concept a lot of thought."

She agreed that she was – she couldn't understand why I was talking so much about promptness. Her clients typically waited several hours for service. "But, so what? Why should we have to speed up the process? I just don't see the point. They don't have anywhere else to go anyway."

The Science of Service

Seconds passed as my mind raced. How could she think that her clients' time was irrelevant? Because they were *poor*?

I asked her, "When you are not at work, you still have a long list of things to get done each day, right? Grocery shopping, dry cleaning, things like that?" She nodded. "When you are out doing your own thing, is your time valuable?" Now the entire class nodded, some emphatically. They were starting to get it. Respect includes respecting other people's time.

I wanted to relay that, in spite of the fact the customers didn't have the same quality of life as the workers, their time was just as precious. I asked, "If you lost your job and needed public assistance just to eat, what other problems would you likely be experiencing?" Answers included lack of childcare, transportation problems, housing problems, medical problems and more. I said, "That's a lot of stress, and a lot of difficulty to navigate all at once. Do you think people in this position might be struggling to accomplish basic things? Might this put them under considerable time constraints?"

In this light, the people in class quickly became less judgmental and much more empathetic about their customers. This is a pivotal shift – the roots of respect.

Once you embrace the idea that everyone deserves respect, showing respect is simple and easy.

In person, always greet customers when they come in. Thank them for coming in. Make eye contact. Smile. Use warm, friendly voice tones. If you are serving other customers or are on the phone, take a moment to acknowledge visitors in a non-verbal way.

On the phone, respect is conveyed through your tone of voice. Empathy and willingness to help can be heard in a heartbeat; so can distractedness, impatience and irritation. To give the right impression: 1) focus on the caller; 2) give a professional greeting; 3) avoid distractions such as glancing at e-mails during the call.

When e-mails are exchanged, people sense respect by the structure of your message. E-mails should include a greeting ("Dear Mr. Smith") and a signature block with your name, title, department and phone number. It's nice to include a closing statement such as, "Please feel free to contact me if you have any questions or need additional information." These details show the recipient that you took a little extra time to be professional and thorough; it tells the reader, *You Matter.*

When your customer brings a problem, concern or complaint to your attention, that is perhaps the best opportunity to show respect. After listening carefully, thank the person. Yes, *thank him or her.* For every person with a complaint, there could be 100 more who noticed the same thing and never told you. "Complainers" are doing you a huge favor by delivering an opportunity to really make a difference. So, thank them for taking time out of their busy days to give you the chance to fix their problems.

2. Control
Most people don't like to be told what to do. Take children, for example. If a child is coloring and you point your finger and say sternly, "You have to keep coloring. I mean it. Don't you stop until I tell you to," coloring is the last thing that child will want to do. From that moment on, all he or she will think about is when he or she can stop this torturous coloring! Adults are the same way, and when they interact with the government, they can feel just like a child does when controlled by an authority figure.

With so many laws and regulations that govern the services, programs and activities of government, most of the interactions we have with our customers are regulatory or enforcement in nature. We find ourselves telling people what to do, pointing out what they are doing wrong and penalizing them for oversights. No wonder they don't look forward to our smiling faces. They likely feel bossed around.

As service professionals, we're in a position to make their experiences much more palatable. One way to do that is by giving control back to the customer. How? By offering options.

For example, if they have to fill out X application for X permit, could they do it online? Or download a PDF and mail it in? Fax it? E-mail it? Can they make an appointment or call you if they need assistance? These options may seem small but they make a big difference to the customer.

Examine your job function and look for ways to offer options to your customers. By giving customers choices in how they meet requirements, we can prevent people from getting upset or help calm someone who is already upset.

3. Understanding

When you have a problem, the last person you want to talk to is someone who doesn't care or understand your situation. The essence of good service is showing concern and taking the responsibility to help the customer.

Unfortunately, this sense of concern and responsibility is completely lacking in the customer service robots who simply show up and behave "properly." Vacant eyes, a plastic smile and placating comments are not the same as actually giving a darn.

Angry, rude and frustrated people calm down very quickly when they finally feel like someone understands their position and wants to help. So, how do you show real understanding? It's all about empathy. Empathy means acknowledging and understanding that a person's situation is difficult without pitying him or her.

> *Angry, rude and frustrated people calm down very quickly when they finally feel like someone understands their position and wants to help.*

This is easier said than done. When you hear the same stories over and over for weeks, months or even years, it's normal to build walls around your heart and mind to protect yourself from the customers' difficult situations and painful stories. Otherwise, how could you function?

When you start feeling indifferent or judgmental, pretend to be talking to someone you know. For example, if an elderly lady is telling you a story, pretend it's your grandma talking. This will bring understanding and caring back into your voice and changes your demeanor, facial expressions, tone, even the words you choose. (According to my students, this is a very helpful technique.)

4. Resolution

As we all know, most of our customers don't jump out of bed and think, "Oh yay, today I get to drive to city hall and stand in line to pay for my building permit!" On the contrary, they wake up groaning, already anticipating an uncomfortable, costly, lengthy, "I'd rather be doing anything else" kind of day. The truth is interacting with a government agency is just like any other chore or task – the sooner it's over, the better.

In addition to providing respect, control and understanding, the kindest thing you can do for your customers is make the process as quick as possible. After all, everyone wants to be finished with his or her chores.

Work with your team to streamline processes, decrease wait times and improve decision making. For example, you could institute an appointment option for first-timers who might have more questions than experienced customers. Or, you could post Frequently Asked Questions and Answers (FAQs) on the website. Or perhaps an educational "on hold" message could answer some questions before a live representative takes the call.

Do what you can to move your customers to the finish line faster.

What is good service? And what makes it great?

If we keep our minds on exactly what our job is, "customer service" becomes a lot clearer and easier.

We come to work every day **to be of service.** That includes both:
- ▶ Providing the required task, information or action
- ▶ The *way* you provide it

In other words, it's not only *what* you do but *how* you choose to do it. These are equally important.

We've all heard the phrase "attitude is everything," and honestly, when it comes to customer service, it is. If someone hates his or her job and doesn't want to be there, that comes across to the customers. If someone is a pessimistic, lazy or negative person, that comes across, too. And, if a person is inherently cheerful, that becomes a part of your customers' experiences.

Therefore, we must do our best to hire people with great attitudes and then ensure they have the necessary technical accuracy. After all, most of my technical training was gained on the job – through mentors and teachers or research and development – even though I have a master's degree! I *wanted* to learn. I *wanted* to be great at work. I had a "bring it on" attitude and so do all of my greatest co-workers.

When interviewing people for a position, all things being equal, go for the person with the best attitude. You can teach him or her the job but it is almost impossible to teach someone basic character traits like how to care. You can't train a person's outlook on life. That's what therapists are for not supervisors.

> *You can't train a person's outlook on life. That's what therapists are for not supervisors.*

In government, there are civil service rules on hiring, rules on who to interview and rules for how you rate each candidate. There may be specific questions you have to ask. That shouldn't stop you from looking for signs of a candidate's attitude. It will shine through in the stories they tell and their demeanor, and the answers they give when you ask situational questions. Remember, a great attitude is the genesis of great service.

In the private sector, these two aspects of customer service – what you do and how you do it – contribute to customer satisfaction, loyalty, revenue, brand integrity and a host of other

Key Performance Indicators (KPIs) that are less relevant in the government sector.

Are government customers always going to be satisfied with the outcome of our interactions? Probably not. Just ask the restaurant manager holding a Notice of Violation for improper food handling. Measuring only his or her satisfaction with the outcome of the situation is not going to indicate much about the quality of service that the enforcing officers provided.

So, what customer service KPIs should public employees focus on?

Three Core Components of High-Quality Customer Service

Instead of overall customer satisfaction, government employees must focus on and assess *the quality of the service delivered,* reflected by three core components:
- ▶ Courtesy
- ▶ Knowledge
- ▶ Promptness

COURTESY

No matter what your role or situation, courtesy is 100 percent within your control. It includes professionalism in appearance and manner, how you relate to other people, body language and demeanor, sense of humor, kindness and caring. These qualities make a lasting impression on people and contribute to the reputation of the entire organization.

For those of us who answer the same questions every day, one of our biggest "occupational hazards" is fatigue. It's not easy to stay fresh, helpful and courteous when you repeatedly encounter people who are frustrated, impolite, dishonest or defensive. Many of us become jaded, naturally.

While this may be understandable, it is regrettable and preventable. As soon as a service provider becomes jaded, he or she loses interest in courtesy – and every other aspect of providing great customer service. If we don't challenge ourselves to withhold judgment and try to see the best of human nature instead of the worst, our discontent will surely grow.

It is easier to do this kind of work when you maintain a positive outlook. But don't expect your department to provide any training on these issues – few do. It is up to you, as an individual or supervisor, to actively bolster yourself and those around you with attitude adjustments, emotional support, values reinforcement, coaching, motivation and modeling. Focusing on the big picture, "The Noblest Motive is the Public Good" always helps me refocus.

KNOWLEDGE
The level of service you provide is largely determined by your ability to answer a question correctly the first time it is asked. This may seem straightforward but providing accurate knowledge can be like hitting a moving target. It requires work on your part.

With the passage of new laws and regulations, our jobs change – and so do the answers to our customers' questions. In addition, our internal policies and procedures could change at any time. Keeping pace can be time-consuming and requires effort.

For front-line staff, this is usually coordinated at a higher level and disseminated through staff meetings, training sessions, e-mails, brown bags, memos and so on. Supervisors and managers have the responsibility of gathering this information (or making sure someone else does).

However, that is only the beginning. As we all know, there are two types of decisions we make as public servants: ministerial and discretionary. Ministerial decisions are black and white: if X, then Y. Period. If you are going to move more than 200 cubic yards of dirt, you need a grading permit. Period.

The hard part is the discretionary decisions. These are, by far, the vast majority of the decisions we make, and they come in all shades of gray. This can be a huge problem for the customer.

When three different people interpret the same situation three different ways, the customer's progress stalls.

When a department has a high turnover rate or many new hires (as we often see in high-stress, front-line, high-contact jobs), customers are most vulnerable. Budget cuts also threaten performance as formal training programs are replaced by tribal learning. Tribal learning is prevalent in government service – you learn by oral communications. If you have a great supervisor/mentor, you learn. If you have someone who is just going through the motions, you may not get all the information you need to be successful.

When employees are hired, they usually have an orientation that ranges from a few hours to a few days. They learn about employee benefits and retirement packages, and how to perform the specific tasks they were hired to do. Then they are paired with a more experienced worker for the on-the-job training. Again, this usually focuses on how to perform certain tasks. The quality of this training can vary tremendously depending on:

- ▶ The expertise of the trainer
- ▶ The attitude and open-mindedness of the trainer
- ▶ The availability of manuals and written documentation

While tribal training may include tips on working with customers, it usually fails to:

- ▶ Define great service
- ▶ Set expectations of great service
- ▶ Emphasize the importance of providing that type of service every day

These are fundamental holes in the knowledge base of any employee. If we don't properly train on where the bar is set and how to consistently meet – *even exceed* – expectations, how can we possibly develop a strong culture of service?

The Science of Service

PROMPTNESS

Good service is fast service. Our customers want to know *when* they can expect results. They *need* to know. And, they need you to be consistently prompt with your communication and actions.

- ▶ Return calls and e-mails within 24 hours or the next business day
- ▶ Provide timelines and updates to your customers
- ▶ Use an "away" message on e-mail and voicemail when you'll be away for a day or more, and include an alternate contact

You could say that government customers have an even higher expectation of promptness because:

- ▶ They are convinced that the process will be laborious and cumbersome
- ▶ They arrive anxious to "get on with it" and they often have a lot waiting on the processes we facilitate

As mentioned before, streamlining processes is a critical component of promptness – but the human factor may be even more influential. Make a personal commitment to be prompt and get similar commitments from your team.

The A-Factor: Attitude

No matter how courteous, knowledgeable or prompt you are, there's one last ingredient that ties it all together to create a world-class customer service experience: ATTITUDE!

To provide great service, we have to "own" a commitment to excel in these three areas (courtesy, knowledge and promptness), and to deliver them as best we can, every day, with every contact.

When this commitment is made by an entire team, department or organization, the results are exponential. Here are some ways to foster that:

▶ **Assess attitudes at the hiring table.** With skill sets being equal, always choose the person with a more positive, can-do attitude. This is so important. Customer service is all about attitude. You can teach someone a job but you can't change his or her basic nature.

In addition to attitude, assess a candidate's team orientation and customer service experience by asking open-ended questions such as, "Tell us about a time you assisted a difficult customer and what skills helped you the most."

One lady told her interviewer that she was "a people person," committed to providing great service throughout her career. Good start. Then she proceeded to share about the difficult co-workers she had to *deal with* (internal customers) and how they were the *worst* because they were so demanding and expected her to drop everything and help them. "Once someone got upset with me, and I told him that he wasn't my only customer, and I'd get to him when I got the chance." This was her idea of being a people person.

A person's attitude ripples through every decision, every task, the quality of every effort, how they see the world and what they think is right and wrong. Hiring people with great attitudes puts the entire department on track to create a sustainable culture of great service.

▶ **For every job posted include "great customer service skills" with the list of qualifications;** it is a critical skill required to succeed and the statement sets the candidate up with the right expectations for the job. (Note: This may or may not be a union meet-and-confer issue; this is generally not considered a change in expectations but a documentation of expectations that already exist.)

- ▶ **Include basic customer service training with every new-employee orientation.** Along with the usual information on the organization, benefits and retirement plans, new employees should know the minimum expectations in service.
- ▶ **Create a formal document that details basic customer service standards** and distribute copies to every new employee as well as existing staff.

Lessons from the Front Lines: When You Have to Say 'No'

Customer service in government is different from customer service in the private sector. Most experts look at great customer service as the customer being "satisfied" with the end result. That might work in retail but in government, a customer's satisfaction with the outcome could be quite low – even when the service was stellar.

The government, in its most fundamental purpose, exists to enforce the law and protect public health and safety. Because much of government work involves enforcing laws and regulations, we have to say "no" a lot. There are classes that are specific to this but here are some basic strategies:

- ▶ **Lesson #1: Ask enough questions** so you understand what the customer really wants or needs. Listen closely to understand better. You might be able to offer a do-able alternative that the customer didn't even know existed and would also meet his or her needs.
- ▶ **Lesson #2: Your customers are not process experts – you are.** It isn't fair to think of customers as "uneducated" and act put out when the customer doesn't know the right questions to ask. If you went in for a medical procedure, would you necessarily know all the right questions to ask? Or, would you rely on the doctors and nurses to know what matters and help fill in the blanks? You'd want help through the process, no matter how difficult it was to face the technical information.

People are apprehensive about the unknown but a clear explanation can be a huge step in gaining trust. Take a moment to walk your customers through the process and point out information that you feel would be helpful in their unique situations even if they didn't know to ask.

> ▶ **Lesson #3: Extend a hand and build a bridge.** Let people know you are in this together and that you care about their outcomes.

Example: Providing high-quality service even with a difficult outcome.

A local couple wants to build a guesthouse on their property which sits on a large lot so their elderly mother can live with them. They want to give mom her independence and privacy but keep her close enough to care for her.

Because their neighbors have guesthouses on their large properties, the couple decides to hire an architect, spend a lot of money and then bring their plans to build a guesthouse of their own to the zoning department for approval.

The zoning department employee discovers the property is not zoned for a second dwelling and thinks, *Darn. How do I tell these people the answer is no?*

"I'm so sorry. Even though your neighbors have guesthouses, your particular property is not zoned for a second unit."

The customer starts to get really upset really fast. "What do you mean? We've already spent a lot of money on this, and my mom has already sold her house and is moving out here! I don't care if we can't do it, we're going to do it anyway!"

Here is a brief selection of bad responses:
> ▶ *"Don't get mad at me because you made a mistake."*
> ▶ *"You should have checked with us before you spent the money."*
> ▶ *"If you build that house, you will be fined."*

Here is a better alternative:

"I know this must be very upsetting, and I apologize for the inconvenience. Let's talk a few more minutes and I'll see if I can figure something out. Tell me more about what features you would like for your second dwelling....Thank you. Okay. I have an alternative for you that will meet your needs in another way. You can build an accessory apartment; it's a separate living space that is attached to your home by one wall. That way, your mother can move out here, have her privacy and be close to family. The plans will need to be updated if you decide you'd like to pursue this idea but it's a relatively simple process. Here's a brochure explaining how to permit this type of project. My name is Marco, and you can call me or visit again if you have any questions or concerns."

Notice the distinction: that's high-quality service – courteous, prompt and knowledgeable – even with a difficult customer.

If our customers are in fact satisfied with their results, that is icing on the cake; but that is not necessarily the goal. In this case, although the solution was not what the customer originally wanted, he was in fact satisfied with the outcome.

Oftentimes, employees who are heavily enforcement-oriented are skeptical about incorporating customer service principles into their work. This skepticism is usually tied to the idea that great customer service can only be measured by customer satisfaction.

I used to fall for that idea, too. In fact, when I was the new Customer Service Manager for the County of San Diego, I wondered aloud if I should call my program the "Customer Satisfaction Center" or "Customer Service Center." A seasoned colleague peered over the rim of her glasses and said sarcastically, "Honey, if you call it customer satisfaction, you are setting yourself up to fail."

> **When we focus on the quality of the service delivery, we embody respect for the office we hold and the people we serve.**

She was right. (Well, half-right.) In government, we focus on the quality not the outcome. When we focus on the quality of the service delivery, we embody respect for the office we hold and the people we serve.

At the same time, customers should always be satisfied that you did your best to help them regardless of the outcomes. They should always feel that you were courteous, professional, kind, knowledgeable and prompt. They should always walk away feeling that you genuinely cared and did your best. That is a satisfying customer service...even when they aren't happy about paying the required fee.

Satisfaction Is In The Eye Of The Beholder

Customer satisfaction is quite subjective. While one person may think you are fabulous, another might find you aloof or rude, or worse. As a customer service professional, I focus on how to make a great impression on every person every day, and I think I do a pretty good job at that. But, what does it matter what I think? I could go around all day patting myself on the back (and sometimes I do), but it doesn't amount to a hill of beans if my customers don't feel that I'm serving them well!

> **Everyone is like a snowflake.**

Every person you come in contact with is unique. This is my "Everyone is like a snowflake" theory. Everyone is different from every other customer. Consider the mix of nationalities, languages, religious beliefs, generations, levels of education, skills, personalities and perspectives. Depending on personal history and place of origin, many have preconceived notions of fear and secrecy about the government.

The Science of Service

Here's an example of how different people may interpret the same situation differently because of their own inherent differences. Have you ever gone to a movie with someone, and they walked out raving about the movie while you thought it was mediocre? It happens all the time because "everyone is a snowflake."

The key to providing great service is to quickly assess each individual customer as far as what great service would look like to him or her. While every customer wants courteous, knowledgeable, and fast service, different people have different ideas of what that means.

For example, Pete is 85 years old. Like many people his age, he prefers to conduct his business by phone not e-mail. If Pete leaves a voicemail with a question and you get back to him by e-mail, he won't see that as good service no matter how fast or knowledgeable your answer was. Why? Because he called you; he expects a call back. Maybe he only checks his e-mail once a week. If he doesn't see your response for a week, you have failed to provide courteous and prompt service.

On the other hand, Dao-Ming is 16 years old and has a cell phone with her at all times. She prefers to communicate via text. E-mails take too long!

Great service first recognizes customers as people, looks for what they need then delivers the three core components of great service – courtesy, promptness and knowledge.

How to Satisfy Customers – Before You Ever Meet Them

Good news! There are many ways to ensure customers have positive experiences before they even meet a staff member.

The experience a customer has with an organization is made up of both direct and indirect contacts.

Direct service is the human interaction between the government employee and the citizen, customer or client. This interaction is usually in person or via telephone or e-mail.

Indirect service points and white space include all the points at which a customer forms a perception of your department before he or she ever speaks with an employee. It could be the form letter your office sent or the automated phone system.

Maximize impressions of the white space.

One of the factors that makes a strong (often negative) impression on customers is known as white space. This term describes the space where something isn't, and it greatly influences how someone interprets what is there. This is a subset of the indirect impressions people have of service during the course of attempting to conduct that service.

In your work, white space is the time between the moments when an employee is working directly with a customer. Here's an example.

▶ Your customer has to visit your office at lunchtime to pick up some forms so she drives to your building and finds no parking (white space) near the entrance because everyone else is visiting at lunchtime, too. She parks in the lot and walks toward the building (white space).

▶ She gets to the entrance and enters a long gray corridor (white space).

▶ In the lobby, she sees many different counters with signs hanging from the ceiling (Zoning, Building, Plan Check, Land Use, Small Water Systems and more). After reading them all and choosing a line (white space), she counts the customers in line ahead: six. *Sigh.* (More white space.)

Before the customer service provider even says hello, the white space has already left a negative impression of your department. This makes it difficult for the employee to make a great

The Science of Service

impression on the customer. Talk about getting stuck behind the eight ball!

All of these customer impressions contribute to your office's reputation. This concept has been examined in-depth by service gurus such as Jan Carlzon, former CEO of Scandinavian Airlines, who discusses "moments of truth." Every point of contact, either direct or indirect, becomes an impression stored in memory.

However, this doesn't have to be the end of the story. When your exasperated, frazzled customer finally makes it to your window, you greet her with a big smile and great attitude, ready to help and eager to do everything right.

It is in the best interest of every organization to manage the white space to the best of its ability. One of the best ways to do this is to "mystery shop" a facility and examine both the indirect and direct impressions. Then do your best to improve both, as they both have impact to the impressions you are making on every person, every day.

Personal Benefits For Great Service Providers

First, a few quick questions:
- ▶ Do you hate to get yelled at all day?
- ▶ Are you sick of hearing "you only work in government because you can't get a real job"?
- ▶ Are you tired of working for an organization that attracts negative comments?

If the answer to any (or all) of those questions is "yes," great news! You are now equipped with the ability to single-handedly change these things.

The perception each person has of government and of any agency in particular is made up of a lot of moving parts including media portrayals, scandals, experiences with other agencies and more. The good news is that YOU are part of that perception.

Every single time you answer the phone, send an e-mail or stand behind a government counter, *you are the government* to your customers. All of these one-time impressions add up to form the overall reputation of the government – not just your department or your agency but all of government.

"The Government" is big and confusing. With so many departments and agencies, even government workers aren't always aware of other departments and programs within their own agency let alone other agencies. If employees have trouble with it, how can a member of the public be expected to sort it out?

If your customer was to hear a negative news story about your agency, we want him or her to say, "Huh, that's strange. I've worked with that agency. The employees treated me fairly, gave quick answers and knew how to guide me through complicated processes. I don't believe that negative story."

What if your customers were so impressed with your service that they defended your organization to their family and friends? What if they spoke *highly* of your work and caring and commitment to help them get through the process? What would happen then? Look off in the distance. Is that the tide of public opinion turning in your favor?

YOU are powerful. YOU have the power to change someone's opinion. By making great impressions, day in and day out, YOU can change public opinion, one person at a time.

> *To laugh often and much;*
> *To win the respect of intelligent people and the affection of children;*
> *To earn the appreciation of honest critics*
> *and endure the betrayal of false friends;*
> *To find the best in others; to leave the world a bit better,*
> *Whether by a healthy child, a garden patch*
> *or a redeemed social condition;*
> *To know even one life has breathed easier because you have lived.*
> *This is to have succeeded.*
> *- Attributed to Ralph Waldo Emerson*

Chapter Two

Building a Culture of Service
with Six Essential Elements
(and a Lynchpin)

Give me a lever and a place to stand,
and I can move the world.
- Archimedes

Knowing what great service is and consciously deciding that it is your job to be great at customer service is completely up to each individual. The systems we put in place to support a culture of service are a very effective lever but it's the individual who must choose his or her personal position.

In every organization, government or otherwise, there are pockets of great employees with great leaders and pockets of lukewarm people. In a perfect world, all people in positions of authority would recognize that putting effort into establishing a culture of service would benefit everyone – internal and external customers alike.

Early in my management career, a supervisor told me that it's the manager's responsibility to buffer the team from what happens outside the team. In this case, "buffer" meant creating a sphere of influence with certain expected behaviors and a stable atmosphere regardless of what was going on in other areas of the department or organization.

When great customer service is the expectation, any good leader knows that if you take care of your people, your people will take care of the customers. Unfortunately, many managers follow the philosophy that "beatings will continue until morale improves."

They use their power and influence over others to control for the sake of control, not empowering the staff and providing them with opportunities and challenges for professional growth.

Foster "spheres of influence." If a customer-focused culture is to be infused into your organization, the first thing you need is to foster "spheres of influence" throughout the organization. This is a grassroots effort. There will be people who quickly embrace the ideals and run with them, others will have a "wait and see" approach.

The second thing you need is a plan.

When I became the Customer Service Manager for the County of San Diego, I had an unusual skill set for my role. With a Master's of Science in Public Health, I brought a scientific mindset to the job which gave me the ability to design a plan to conduct experiments and test hypotheses in a way that followed a scientific method. While creating a customer-focused culture may have been a soft science before, it's not anymore. Now there is a step-by-step approach that will successfully infuse change into any organization.

Six Essential Elements to Create a Culture of Service

Exceptional organizations have an infrastructure or system in place to develop the culture and improve standards of customer service whether or not that infrastructure has been named a "customer service program." The infrastructure is composed of six essential elements.

1) Set expectations and customer service standards
2) Train staff
3) Empower and value staff, and include them in the success of the organization
4) Measure success and gather customer feedback
5) Reward and recognize people who meet and exceed expectations

The Science of Service

6) Improvement projects – repair and/or remove any obstacles to great service

Each of these areas will be explored in-depth in the coming chapters but for now it's helpful to paint a big-picture view of this plan so it's clear where, how and why all these pieces fit together.

The Lynchpin of Great Customer Service: Fully-engaged Staff

If the Six Essential Elements are the gears to run the "Great Customer Service Machine," the machine requires operators – people who fire it up and keep it running smoothly.

At the core of any customer-centric culture are the employees. They must feel valued by the organization and their colleagues. They must understand on a deep level that their team sees them as individuals with a valid contribution to make. They must see the duties they perform as essential to the overall success of the organization. They have to believe *they matter.*

The number one reason people leave jobs is not about the pay. It's because they feel like they don't matter. It is the responsibility of an organization to not only "get the work done" but also to feed this fundamental human need in the employees. When employees truly feel like they matter, the loyalty, extra effort, synergy, accomplishments and more are multiplied in immeasurable ways. When there's a "fusion reaction" within a working group, there is absolutely no stopping them.

When there's a "fusion reaction" within a working group, there is absolutely no stopping them.

In a customer-focused culture, people aim to be more inclusive, good listeners, fair, objective, honest, intelligent, caring and trustworthy. They have the best interests of the team and organization at heart. If you're thinking, "I want that! I want to be a part of that team," let's look at how to develop a stronger, more caring team.

Guideline # 1: **Everyone has value, and if you want to keep your staff engaged, you must show that in both action and word.** No job is more or less important. The director is not more important than the front-line people. There is a reason each job exists, and there is a way to tie the accomplishments of the individual to the accomplishments of the team. Fundamentally value others and recognize the significance of their contributions to the overall team.

When I started my career as a student intern, there were several people who mentored and coached me, took me under their wings and helped me acclimate. They treated me as if my tasks were important and continually put me in situations where I could succeed and grow.

Then there was Jim (not his real name), a self-important manager who saw only a lowly student when I passed by. He wouldn't even look at me in the halls, and I was very uncomfortable around him.

Here's the point: we have a powerful influence on the people around us. If your boss was like my mentor, how would you feel about your work and value? If your boss was like Jim, how would you feel about your work and value? Would you behave differently?

Be a positive influence on those around you whenever you can.

Guideline # 2: **Communication is key in creating a culture of service.** Keep your people informed. As I said before, if you take care of your people, they will take care of your customers. It's so common to whisper and keep things a secret... big things, small things, important things and insignificant things. It's destructive and counterproductive. Take steps to be as honest and up-front as possible, sharing all you know that can be shared. (Obviously, some things are confidential... investigations and personnel matters, for example... but really, not as much as people tend to protect.)

For example, budget cuts: Shhh.... Whatever you do, don't tell the staff. They will just get all upset. Go figure out your cuts and we'll decide at the management meeting.

Well, that's one approach but certainly not the only one.

What if everyone sat down together to discuss the coming changes and share their ideas? People will not necessarily agree with each other but there would be no back-alley deals or gossipy subterfuge just an open collaboration that could benefit everyone. In the end, the leader makes the decision. Everyone will not agree but you've just gone a long way to establish trust and respect in your team.

During a recent exercise with a group of 15 front-line staff and supervisors, it quickly came to light that poor communication from management to staff was the biggest problem. The staff knew they could do their jobs better if only they knew what was going on around them and could coordinate their efforts through regular meetings and more informative e-mails. Could this be true in your organization, too?

Set up a communications strategy that includes the following items:
- ▶ Regular staff meetings (invite people to participate on the agenda)
- ▶ Periodic visits with your team at their location(s)
- ▶ E-mailed updates regarding significant or interesting department news
- ▶ Periodic all-staff voicemails

Perhaps the most important part of your communications strategy is this: be human. Show your own caring side and it will inspire your team to show theirs as well.

Guideline # 3: **Practice Rumor Control.** Talking negatively about co-workers and colleagues will unravel the strength of your group. Rumors, cliques and gossip are extremely destructive. A customer-focused culture puts its foot down on how we treat each other and how we communicate the truth. It goes without saying but it's important enough to emphasize: *do not gossip or speak poorly of others in the organization or even in other organizations.* Be the model of the behaviors you would like to see in others.

The higher up in an organization you get, the less in touch you are with the guts of the organization. What you know to be true as a manager and what your people are saying can be two very different things. What are the rumors about the budget, performance measures, staffing and operations? It's your job to know what's really going on, and the only way you can is to be honest and up-front.

If you have a reputation for proactive communication, people tend to believe you and trust you. If you create an environment where you are open to hearing things that you may not agree with, people will tell you what they are thinking. If you create an environment where people can come to you and tell you things they've heard, they will.

When you hear gossip, rumors or divisive talk, confront it head on. Tell your team what you are hearing, what the facts are and what the unknowns are. This type of direct communication keeps the team on track, moving forward and united.

Chapter Three
Essential Element One: Setting Expectations

Consider the many ways that employees might contact a customer, either directly or indirectly. Every point of contact leaves a lasting impression of you, the organization, and government in general – and the goal is to make every impression a good one. However, it is unfair to tell an employee to be good at something without first defining what "good" means in the eyes of the organization.

Each employee comes from a different upbringing, ethnicity, value set, town, state, country... not to mention one of the five generations currently working together! Each employee is a snowflake just like our customers.

Assume the same disparities exist among your team members. In order to set them up for success, it is crucial to provide written best practices and expectations for great service. Use the following standards as a starting point for your standards and best practices document. Feel free to customize this list to your unique work environment and add specifics where appropriate.

Making Great Impressions and Providing Great Service

In Person

▶ **Be aware of the neatness of your attire.** First impressions, including how professionally you are dressed, make an immediate impact on your customer. Your customers' attitude toward you, and therefore your ability to assist them quickly and accurately, is affected by how you present yourself. If your customer recognizes you as a professional, his or her demeanor will be more positive than if you create the impression that you don't care.

- ▶ **Greet people when they enter your area.** If you are busy with another customer or on the phone, use a non-verbal signal such as making eye contact, nodding and smiling.
- ▶ **Smile and be friendly.** While many government customers would rather be somewhere else, pressed for time, annoyed, confused, nervous, unsure where to go or all the above, a simple friendly greeting can immediately put them at ease. Establish a bridge between you and the newcomer, making that person less anxious and annoyed when the time comes to work with you.
- ▶ **Use open, neutral body language and a friendly, approachable facial expression toward customers.** Show respect and treat them with dignity regardless of whether they are a multi-million dollar builder or a single mother getting food stamps. We speak volumes with our body language and gestures before ever saying a word. In fact, studies show that up to 55 percent of our interpersonal communication comes through body language, gestures and facial expressions.[1]

On the Phone

- ▶ **Answer the phone by the third ring.** If you step away from your desk, use call-forwarding. It's frustrating and a waste of time to call and listen to a phone ringing only to finally get routed to voicemail.
- ▶ **If you are out of the office for a day or more, change your outgoing voicemail message.** Include your date of return and an alternate contact in your absence.
- ▶ **Focus on your greeting.** State your name, company name and offer to assist. For example: "Customer Service Department, this is Wendi. How may I help you?" ("Hello," is perfectly fine for home but not for work.)
- ▶ **Be sound-conscious.** Do not eat, chew gum, read e-mails or listen to the radio while speaking with a customer.

---

[1] Dr. Albert Mehrabian authored the 7%-38% 55% rule, indicating the ratio of communication conferred by words, tone and body language (when expressing feelings or attitude).

The Science of Service

Via E-mail

▶ **Use greetings, closings and contact information, as if you were writing a letter** to be printed on letterhead. Good choices are "Dear Sir/Madam, Dear Ms. Smith, etc." and "Sincerely" as a closing. Contact information refers to your signature block including phone number, mailing address, website and/or other relevant information.

Because it is frequently used in a personal context (at home), people tend to be much too informal in their professional e-mails. It is especially important to use a formal style if you are conversing with someone with a higher rank, someone in the organization you do not know or an external customer.

▶ **Emoticons (such as :-) to indicate a smile) are not appropriate in formal correspondence.**

▶ **Be conservative with content. Humor is easily misconstrued.** For example, what if you received this e-mail? *"Nice pants."* How would you interpret that? There are at least three different interpretations (can you identify all three?)– and that message only had two words! Think twice before including anything you intend as humorous and certainly anything of a political or personal nature. To be on the safe side, assume that anyone in the organization may end up seeing your e-mail. (Messages are easily forwarded and can cause much embarrassment even disciplinary action.)

▶ **Remember, e-mails are a permanent record.** They can be, and often are, subpoenaed for court cases. As a general rule: do not write anything in an e-mail you wouldn't want to see as a headline in your local newspaper.

▶ **Write a descriptive subject line.** If you are asking someone to do something, especially with a due date, make it obvious by including it in the subject line. People scroll through e-mails and unless something catches their eye, they may miss the information. A poor subject line might be "Info," while a better one might be, "Report on Wetlands – comments due Friday."

▶ **If you are out of the office, use the auto-reply feature of your e-mail program.** Include your date of return and an alternate contact in your absence. The message should be composed in a formal style like the sample below.

Dear Sir or Madam:
Thank you for contacting the [name of the organization, department]. I will be out of the office this week, and will return on [day of the week], [month, day].

If this is urgent, please contact [first and last name] at [phone number] or via e-mail at [e-mail address]. Otherwise, I will return your e-mail when I am back in the office.

Sincerely,
[first and last name], [title]
[Department]
[phone number]
[Optional: Department mission statement, vision statement, etc.]

In the Field

▶ **Be mindful of the neatness and cleanliness of uniforms and trucks.** These details reflect on the organization.
▶ **Be polite, hold doors, smile and be friendly.** Anyone you meet during the day could be your next customer!
▶ **Follow all traffic laws.** Follow the speed limit, use signals and drive politely.

Unstaffed Sites

Many public organizations are responsible for sites that are staffed intermittently as with parks or open-space preserves. The following tips could also apply to a visitor's first approach to your building or when someone is away from the front counter for a moment.

- ▶ **Use clear signage.** This is a common and easily-fixed problem in many, many locations. Walk-through a visit to your office from the perspective of someone who has never been there. Or, ask a student intern or family member to do a walk-through and report his or her experience.
- ▶ **Make sure the restrooms are clean and well stocked.**
- ▶ **Ensure the equipment and/or facility is clean and safe.** This could include picnic tables, playground equipment, trash cans, water fountains, trails, drop boxes and parking areas, to name a few.

These tips are just the beginning, of course. When creating your standards – host a workshop with the team. Gather the team's input – no one knows how to do a job better than the people doing it! Give this process its due time and attention. After all, these standards are the backbone of your service culture.

Chapter Four

Essential Element Two:
Training Your Team to Provide
Great Service

Effective training is designed according to adult learning theory. It's designed around explanation, demonstration then practice – practice – practice. It's also paced so that every 15 minutes or so there is a high-engagement portion of the training. People can be auditory, visual or kinesthetic learners, and most of us are a combination of all three. A multi-dimensional training ensures that all learners absorb the concepts and, just as important, develop their skills by using the concepts in real-life situations.

No adult will change his or her behavior unless there is a reason to do so. Therefore, the first critical step in training staff to be champions of great customer service is **to give them reasons why this will benefit them directly.**

One reason is that staff can help more people in a given amount of time. Since government is not usually in business to make money, and our internal "economy" often lags behind the regional economy, we are always in cycles of gearing up and cutting back. During the 18 years I've worked in government, six were so economically difficult that there were no raises. Several were bad enough that people lost their jobs. As levels of staffing shift, we can often find ourselves in the familiar position of doing more with less. When you make an effort to excel by offering great service, you can serve more people in the same amount of time. (This was proven by the Technical Assistance Research Project.[2])

---

[2] TARP. 1989

When a customer poses a frequently asked question, it could take on average 2-3 minutes to assist that customer. Given the same question asked by someone who is angry or upset, would it be quicker or take more time to answer?

More time of course! In fact, much more. On average that same interaction would take 10-15 minutes. Why? Because you first have to address the emotion and determine its cause before you can even answer the question. Therefore, if you and your organization are really focused on providing great service, far fewer people will be angry and you will help five times more people with the same number of front-line staff.

Providing great service also makes it more satisfying to come into work every day. No one wants to feel unnecessary or unimportant. Solving people's problems then hearing them say "thank you" is a tremendous boost. You not only solved a puzzle but affected someone else in a positive way.

Success is leaving the world a better place because you existed in it. These small accomplishments can enrich your life to a far greater degree than you can help a customer. In addition, providing genuine caring service to your customers will dramatically decrease stress levels – your own and that of your customers.

Case in point: In October 2003, San Diego County experienced devastating wildfires. There were several burning at once when the wind shifted and fires started raging toward very populated communities. There were mass evacuations and many homes were completely destroyed. I watched the fires cresting over the hills of Daley Ranch, an open space preserve a few miles east of my home. It was surreal and terrifying. Fortunately, that edge of the fire was contained and our community was spared. However, as the Customer Service Manager for the County of San Diego, I was front-and-center to everyone else's tragedies for the next few weeks.

While the fires were still burning, I was called into my boss' office. I was to co-lead an emergency hotline for affected residents and their families to call to see if their homes were still standing after evacuation. I had 24 hours and about 100 volunteers. They were quickly trained in the lunchroom on what resources were to be found where, and how to use the H.E.A.T. method to assist difficult, emotional or angry people. We also trained the team to provide many other resources such as directing people to shelters, taking in volunteers and donated time and materials, and providing critical mental health assistance to victims of the wildfires. We set a schedule and off we went.

The brave and selfless people on the phones did their best, person after person, to help our citizens take the first steps toward stabilization and get their feet back on the ground. The volunteers held up without getting defensive even though we all did cry at one time or another. The customer service training they received made the difference between taking our callers' emotions personally and taking them professionally. We powered through weeks of long days, and I can honestly say it was our training in customer service that got us through.

Use H.E.A.T. to Assist Difficult, Emotional or Angry People

(H) Hear Them Out

When people are very upset or angry, they need some time to vent. If people feel they are not being heard, they tend to raise their voices, talk faster and talk more. Show someone you are really listening and it will reduce his or her stress faster.

Use H.E.A.T. to Assist Difficult, Emotional or Angry People

(E) Empathize

Show caring and concern for each person's situation. It will make him or her feel better and help build a bond between staff and client.

(A) Ask and Answer Questions

We often jump in too quickly, wanting to solve the problem. Make sure you are solving the right problem, and solving it completely, by asking open-ended questions and getting the whole story.

(T) Take Responsibility to Assist

Working with government is daunting. Have you ever opened a phone book and looked at how many government numbers are listed? Finding the right agency, let alone the right person, can leave someone frustrated and anxious. A customer service rep can establish confidence by saying something as simple as, "I know this is complicated. Don't worry, I'm here to help you through the process."

The Science of Service

Chapter Five
Essential Element Three:
Empower Your Team

I recently attended an amazing, passionate meeting about implementing a customer service improvement program. I was just an observer so I had a chance to really listen. A new and innovative project was proposed and its implementation discussed… but it was completely lacking any discussion of change management. There was no plan to communicate the changes to staff, explain why the changes were happening or train them on how to navigate the new guidelines. How could they possibly succeed?

When a new project will affect staff, their work life or how they do business, talk to them about it before you start, during the development and before the deployment. Asking for input from the people who actually do the work always pays off in the long run.

In general, people do not like change – especially change that could make them look bad. They will handle it much better if you empower them with information. Here's how.

Bring the staff together.

Tell them about the new project *before it happens.* Tell them everything about it. Get their input. (Talking to the team – what a concept!)

Discuss how the project will be implemented and when. (All people fear the unknown. In the absence of facts, people make up their own truths.)

Explain how this project will impact the way staff currently work and why the project is needed in the first place.

Train staff so they can be successful under new conditions.

Introducing a new project is a great time to implement a change-management protocol. To be honest, I don't like the term "change management." We're not "managing" change at all. We're proposing great new things, sometimes evolutionary, sometimes revolutionary, and empowering staff to be part of the innovations. By proposing new projects and new ways of doing old things in the organization, we're doing great things even better.

Following these inclusionary practices, we ensure that everyone involved can feel the same pride and sense of accomplishment instead of feeling like something has been done "to" them.

Customer Service for Supervisors

If you take care of your people, your people will take care of your customers.

> *If you take care of your people, your people will take care of your customers.*

Many supervisors are on a power trip or think their job is giving out work assignments. Some have no understanding of their influence over the big picture and it's a crying shame. Organizations are run by first-line supervisors, and these people rise up the ranks to become managers and directors. In my experience, a few are great, most are mediocre and others are just horrible!

So many people suffer under insufferable supervisors; arbitrary decisions are made that negatively affect people's lives with a complete lack of vision and leadership. Laziness and dishonesty drive them to take credit for the staff's work. Rumors, gossip and favoritism run rampant. The list goes on.

What consistently boggles the mind is why people who are higher up in the organization ignore poor supervisors. I knew one supervisor who was so inhumane to the staff, one man had a heart attack, one person was diagnosed with cancer and every single person in the unit had filed a grievance. Yet, it took 2.5 years to replace her. Unbelievable! My question is: why?

The most rewarding part of working could be your opportunity to improve the quality of life of the people on your team. To watch them be challenged and develop new skills. To see them be promoted and excel. To see them smile when they see you because they know you have their best interests at heart.

When I was little, I was very impressed by the character in "A Christmas Carol" named Fezziwig. He was young Scrooge's boss in Christmas Past. In every version of the story, he was happy and generous and acknowledged his staff. They respected and loved him for it.

Scrooge is thankful to Fezziwig, and says, "He has the power to render us happy or unhappy; to make our service light or burdensome; a pleasure or a toil…The happiness he gives is quite as great as if it cost a fortune."

That's important. I'm not saying that you should be friends with your team. (In fact, that could be problematic.) It is paramount, however, that you create an environment where people can grow and contribute, thrive and make mistakes, be supported and see how important they are every day. That's very powerful and that's what you can do as a supervisor.

It's a little different than just handing out work assignments, isn't it?

"I want to be a Fezziwig, too! How does one become a Fezziwig?" That is a great question!

How does one become a Fezziwig?

First step: *want* to be a Fezziwig. If that's the kind of person you want to be, you will seek out models that will teach you to be this way. You will absorb these qualities from others. You will become what you want to become. But if it doesn't seem important or relevant to you, and that's not what you want, you will never be that.

Second step: Make sure the supervisors and managers in your organization have the training and support they need to empower their staff and support a culture of service. If they don't, consider investing in coaches and trainings that guide people to develop a culture of service.

When I became a supervisor for the first time, there was no training available. I lamented that. Someone said to me, "It doesn't matter *why* your staff does what you say, just that they do it."

All these years later, I respectfully disagree. Giants in the field of leadership, like Stephen Covey and Ken Blanchard may also disagree. They and other greats have inspired people to believe in leadership as a means of improving the quality of life for the people in your sphere of influence and the quality of service to your external customers.

Supervisors set the tone for their work group. If your supervisors have strong communications skills, believe in the vision and mission of your organization, and have a deeply-instilled understanding of how they fit in and the value of great service, so will the team. A jaded, burned-out supervisor who is not interested in new ideas and is just collecting a paycheck will have the opposite effect.

I've seen both in my career. It's obvious when you come across pockets of greatness within an organization, and it's usually tied to the leadership skills of the supervisor. Their group always seems optimistic, adaptable, inspiring and fun to be around. Unfortunately, I've also seen the exact opposite.

The Science of Service

When people move from a creative, enthusiastic group to a dull, regimented group, it's really heartbreaking. What a waste of talent. I actually had a former employee call me one day, angry because I used to tell her that I hired her for her brain and if she had something to say she should say it. Her current supervisor didn't care what she thought and didn't want to hear it so she stopped talking. She blamed me for raising her expectations. In a way, I guess it was a compliment but it made me feel so helpless.

A good supervisor realizes that someone can be a leader from anywhere in the organization. Once again, leadership is a choice not a position. You can be a manager without being a leader, and you can be a thought leader on the front line. Rank has nothing to do with it.

A good supervisor knows that people rise to your level of expectation. If you see someone as a star, guess what? They will do everything in their power to be a star. If you see them as talented and creative, yes, they will do their very best to be talented and creative.

In Kurt Mortensen's audio set, *Magnetic Persuasion,* he relays an interesting story about this very topic. This story was about a substitute teacher and a grade-school class. In this class, there was an outstanding student, the "teacher's pet," and a trouble-making class clown. The teacher gave the substitute a rundown on all the information she needed to run the class smoothly, and she mentioned her helper and the trouble-maker. "When you need help, you can always rely on Charlie but watch out for Mikey. He's always sneaking around and getting into trouble."

With so much to remember, the substitute mixed up these two names. She remembered them backwards, believing the trouble-maker was the helper and vice versa. Therefore, that's how she treated them. She kept a suspicious eye on Charlie, watching for anything that might lead to a problem. Every time he got up or looked at another student, she noticed, and Charlie knew she was watching. He got very sneaky with his actions and she disciplined him accordingly.

On the other hand, she treated Mikey like a star. She smiled at him and praised him. She asked for his help and acknowledged how smart and kind he was. She thanked him for being such a great helper and never causing any trouble. And guess what? That's exactly how he behaved.

When the regular teacher returned, she chatted with the substitute to catch-up. She corrected the substitute when she said how wonderful Mikey had been, and how much she appreciated the warnings about Charlie. The teacher was surprised! "You must have gotten the names mixed up. Charlie is the star!" No, the substitute insisted, it was Mikey.

This highlights a valuable lesson for any supervisor or manager: people want to be praised and will go out of their way to do something that will get them noticed. It is up to you to set your expectations and tone accordingly and use sincere praise whenever possible.

Supervisors have tremendous influence over their staff's quality of life. Any good manager knows that if you take care of your people, your people will take care of business. A poor managerial mindset will at best poison, and at worst completely kill an organization's creativity, talent, and the ability to grow, adapt and succeed.

Empowering Staff, Part I:
Helping People Come Out of The CAVE

If you are a great supervisor, it's just as important to know **what not to do** in order to bring out the best in others. The higher up you are in an organization, the more impact your words and actions have on everyone else. Your positional power makes people hear you differently. Therefore, it is absolutely paramount, especially in the nurturing stage of a culture of service, that you think about how your words will be heard by others before you open your mouth. This will do much to promote the culture you desire.

The Science of Service

Case in point: I was teaching a class about (what else?) providing great service. Every class has a bell curve of attendees – 25 percent who are really into what you are saying and love going to training, 50 percent who are middle of the road and pick-up a few tips here and there, and 25 percent that I call "CAVE." people – Citizens Against Virtually Everything (I didn't invent this term but it's perfect!).

I am not too worried about the first 75 percent. If an organization puts in place the Six Essential Elements, those people will likely fall into place and accept the new culture. It's the CAVE people I focus on – and the ones I really like are the ones who are really vocal. I'd rather have people in class who are vocally negative than people who say nothing. People who say nothing are not engaged. They don't care. They have no passion and it's really hard to get those people to play ball.

The CAVE people, however, weren't always CAVE people. Sometime in the past, maybe when they were new to the job, they were probably in the top 25 percent: the leaders, innovators and optimists. Then, something went horribly wrong. They were likely burned by their enthusiasm and experienced a sudden, traumatic shift that told them:

▶ Be quiet
▶ Your opinions don't matter
▶ No one cares about you or your ideas

In my class, one CAVE woman eventually spoke up. She couldn't take all the pointers on providing great service, and blurted out that her clients were "rude and needy. They don't understand that I have other work to do!" She went on along this line a few minutes, scrunching up her face, mimicking her annoying customers and telling me that things weren't really as I portrayed them in the class.

All eyes were glued on her, and I let her vent for a minute. I thanked her for expressing what other people in the class may also be feeling. Then I praised her portrayal of a disengaged employee and thanked her for role-playing it so effectively for the group. Everyone laughed, including her.

A little humor opened her up to listen and see that what I was saying really did apply. Everyone is busy and overwhelmed. It's perfectly natural to have a reaction when customers seem to be interrupting your work… but in reality, aren't your customers the reason for your work? If we had no customers, there would be no job.

When our class CAVE lady expressed frustration at answering the same questions over and over again, we turned the situation around and showed her that if she were to go to an attorney for information about a civil procedure, she might have to ask questions several times before she understood, too. Sometimes people have to ask questions more than once, especially if it's complicated or it's something they never heard before. It's the professional's job to know the process so they can share that information with the customer in a way the customer will understand.

Her final complaint was about people being angry, emotional or "having attitude" while they talked to her. Clearly, it was time to go over the concept of taking this professionally not personally. As gently as I could, I explained, "The person who is upset needs your help. They aren't mad at you; they don't even know you. They are frustrated and angry at the situation, and may even use anger to cover up their embarrassment or fear. If you take a step back and think of yourself as the one person responsible for fixing the problem, you'll have a whole different attitude *yourself*. You will be able to control the situation and resolve it faster."

Soon, she had a smile on her face and was agreeing with the concepts. After class, this young woman approached me and thanked me for the class. She had really learned a lot and was looking forward to practicing her new attitude with her customers. I was thrilled. Those are the "a-ha" moments I live for and why I love teaching these classes. Something really changed in her that day and it was going to make her life better. As a result, she would also provide better service and enhance the success of her career and organization.

When the students had left the room, I looked through the exit surveys with the HR director. We were pleased to see that my loudest critic had become my biggest fan, giving the class the highest rating possible and leaving her e-mail address to subscribe to my newsletter.

Unfortunately, my joy was short-lived. By the time I got back to my office, there was an e-mail from the HR director. I opened it right away.

I soon realized that the e-mail was not to me. I had been blind carbon copied (bcc) on an e-mail from the HR director to the class participant – the one who had the "a-ha" moment that all trainers strive for. Copied on the e-mail were several managers. The message was chastising the participant, shaming her for the honest feelings she had shared.

Now, let's think for a minute: If you are a staff person and you get an irritated e-mail from your HR director, what is your reaction going to be? You're going to crawl right back into your CAVE!

Everything I had said about creating a culture of service and including employees as your customers was lost on this HR director. As soon as he criticized this participant's "a-ha" moment, all her joy and optimism from the class was pulled out from under her like a rug. Her efforts to become a champion of her organization were dashed against the rocks of petty criticism.

Now, I know this HR director and he's actually a very nice man. I'm sure this was not his intent at all, what did we say earlier? Bad service happens through inattention to detail. So does bad supervision. Such a shame.

Exercise: Types of Managers and Their Effects on Staff

Think back on two supervisors from your past, one you really admired and liked, and the other, not so much. What was it that you liked so well? What qualities or characteristics told you they weren't good at being a supervisor? Here are some of the typical responses.

Qualities of a great supervisor:
- ▶ Listens to me
- ▶ Upbeat and happy
- ▶ Truthful and honest
- ▶ Has integrity
- ▶ Explains why
- ▶ Thinks well of me and others
- ▶ Mentors and coaches me
- ▶ Has my back
- ▶ Has an even temperament even when things go wrong
- ▶ Encourages me to be a creative problem-solver

Qualities of a poor supervisor:
- ▶ Operates on hidden agendas
- ▶ Lots of secrets, withholds information
- ▶ Doesn't encourage new thoughts or experimentation
- ▶ Has a temper
- ▶ Doesn't represent the group professionally (in appearance, demeanor or communication skills)
- ▶ Takes credit for the work of others
- ▶ Not interested in the team's input

Take a few moments to think about how these supervisors affected your day-to-day actions. Now, here's the million-dollar question: Which supervisor are you? To find out, you must try to see yourself as your staff sees you not how you see yourself.

This exercise highlights an absolutely critical concept for establishing a culture of service. Every single manager in the organization should be expected to get the work done AND be a great manager. To accomplish that, time must be invested in supporting these people and their objectives (especially first-time supervisors).

The Science of Service

Empowering Staff, Part II:
Helping People OWN Their Part of the Big Picture

Studies repeatedly tell us that people's understanding of their jobs and their functions in organizations affects how they behave, how they treat internal and external customers, their loyalty to the team and their job satisfaction.

Let me give an example.

A student worker is just starting her career with a local government agency. She was given some clerical duties so she filed, entered data and then went home. The next day, she filed. She entered data. She went to lunch. She filed. She entered data. She went home.

Halfway through her summer job, she was out with friends and they asked her about where she worked. She said, "They do something with hazardous materials. I'm not really sure. I know people go out to businesses and update records because when they come back, they pile them on my desk. I enter the data in the database and then I file the paperwork in the central files."

"Oh wow!" her friend smirked. "Could that be any more boring?" They all laughed and she laughed with them. She certainly wasn't going to file papers for the rest of her life!

Now, here's another scenario.

A young student worker just starting her career joined a local government agency. She was placed with a supervisor who was fun and happy to be at work. The supervisor explained the student's job like this:

"This department is really important in protecting public health and the environment. We work as a team to help businesses who use hazardous and toxic materials to do so in a way that's safe for them and safe for the air and water. We have inspectors who go out and educate businesses about safety and legal issues. We hold free workshops and seminars every January, when new laws take effect, and change how businesses operate. We conduct free consultations before official inspections and do our best to help people avoid all violations. But some people do violate the law. We work with them to correct the problems quickly but if they are not compliant, we help the attorneys put a case together to prosecute them for endangering people and the environment.

"You have an important role on our team. You will be responsible for updating the businesses' information each time an inspector goes out and completes an inspection report. They will put the file on your desk. You enter the data in the database and then file the information so we can find it again. The data you enter and the way you file the information is important because later we might need it for a case or for some follow-up with the business. I know it's a lot of responsibility but I can tell you are really smart and I think you can handle it. Are you in?"

Imagine the second student, halfway through her summer job, going out with her friends. She was looking forward to talking about her work. This is what she might have said.

"I had no idea so many people came to work every day to make sure the air and water stays clean, and to protect the health of workers and the public. My team works with businesses that use hazardous materials. My job is to update all the files so we have accurate records and can see trends. My work may also be used in court cases to protect the environment! I really love being there, and I'm thinking about applying for a full-time position in the fall."

Same job, same responsibilities. One student was just there to enter data and collect a paycheck. The second student felt like a critical contributor to the organization's success, and held a higher vision of protecting the world around her.

Do you think those two students had different attitudes at work? Do you think there were differences in their excitement, how they answered the phone, how they represented the organization at meetings and how they influenced others about their organization?

When people understand how they fit in and how their job is part of the bigger picture, it makes all the difference. This is the power of a great supervisor.

This is the power of empowering your people.

Chapter Six
Essential Element Four:
Measurement and Feedback

Are you doing a good job? Well, how do you measure success?

When it comes to creating a culture of service, gathering data is critical. Simply saying you are going to gather data instills the core value that customer service is paramount to the organization. What gets measured is what gets improved.

What you are doing every day is measurable. So is *how* you are doing it, and that's what we capture when we measure the quality of customer service. These quantitative and qualitative measures are driven by your organization's key performance measures (or KPIs).

Gathering data in a regimented fashion instills accountability. People become more aware of the way they are doing things when they know they will be evaluated on what, when and how. So, focus on gathering data that is directly related to your expectations of service and the skills developed through training classes.

Focus on gathering data that is directly related to your expectations of service and the skills developed through training classes.

Alignment is central to any organization – and in many organizations, it's off the mark. Everything should easily roll up and roll down from the vision through the mission, goals and objectives, tasks and key performance indicators. This should be true for every individual in the organization from the CEO to the middle manager to the secretary and maintenance staff. External customers (and looking to private sector businesses) are a valuable source of insights and tips on customer service improvement. People external to your day-to-day routine are looking at the service delivery with fresh eyes, and they compare it with other service experiences they have had. This is true whether their experience was with another government agency, a nonprofit agency or a private company.

I once worked on a project to create an electronic signature for customers to access data online. It was for a government agency, and there were a lot of policy disputes about accepting payment over the Internet. What if there was fraud? How could we ensure accuracy? How could we keep the credit card numbers secure? There were so many meetings and debates and questions! At one point, someone (OK, it may have been me) said, "Look, we're not the first organization to accept a credit card payment over the Internet. Amazon does it a billion times every day. There must be a way we can do it, too."

After all, our customers, government customers, do have lives outside of their transactions with us and they compare their transactions with the government with their transactions in the private sector. That is part of the reason why government customers get so frustrated when things seem overly complicated. It's also the reason they have lots of great ideas on how our service can be improved. Don't be afraid to tap this invaluable resource.

And give your customers lots of ways to provide feedback. It's so much better to make it easy for customers to tell you about problems – and then fix them! Whenever a customer has called me with a concern (complaint), I always start the conversation by saying "Thank you for taking the time to call." Remember, many other people are experiencing the same thing and not telling you. How can you fix what you don't know is wrong?

All About Surveys

There are several ways to gather data; different solutions work well in different environments. Each organization must analyze the pros and cons to see what will work best. Here are a few questions to ask before you begin.

> ▶ Which customer group are we polling? They could be internal or external to your team, department or organization.
>
> ▶ Why are we asking these people if they are satisfied with the service?
>
> ▶ What components of the service are we asking about?
>
> ▶ Are we asking formally or informally?
>
> ▶ Are we asking about a specific contact, a recollection or a general impression?
>
> ▶ Do we have a valid and reliable survey instrument?
>
> ▶ Who is the final report for, and what will they do with the information?
>
> ▶ Do we have someone in the organization designated to administer the survey from "cradle to grave," making copies, coordinating distribution, gathering completed surveys, inputting data and analyzing and reporting the data?
>
> ▶ Did we write everything down step-by-step so the survey is repeatable and conducted exactly the same way every time regardless of who is in charge?

Surveys are worthless if the questions are not formulated correctly or if they do not ask about items that are actionable (meaning: changeable). For example, parking is often a source of frustration to customers. Can you change the parking situation? Probably not, so don't ask people if they are satisfied with the parking. Slow turn-around times are a frequent source of frustration with customers. Can you change internal processes to make them faster? Probably, so asking about the promptness of service is a very good question.

Survey questions should be aligned across different customer groups so there can be an apple-to-apple comparison. If you develop seven standard questions that really get to the heart of the data you want to capture, use them on all the surveys you can. For example, the question about being prompt can be used on a counter survey, a mail-out survey and a variety of mystery-shopping surveys (in person, e-mail and over the phone).

I am not a statistician or a professional survey developer so the surveys I have implemented are not statistically significant, the samples sizes are not calculated and meaningful and no T-testing or Chi-square testing can be performed on the results. You will have to judge whether you need that level of professional support and detail or whether a "quick and dirty" but highly-repeatable experiment will provide enough actionable data to suffice.

To make sure these surveys are useful and give you the information you think they will, follow these guidelines.

Guideline #1: **Surveys should always be documented to the letter and implemented exactly the same way each time they are deployed.** For example, if surveys are placed on public counters every nine months for a two-week period, the next survey should be placed on public counters in nine months for a two-week period. (And the same the time after that.)

If you can change the implementation, be cautioned that results of previous surveys may not be comparable to current and future surveys.

Guideline #2: **Resist the temptation to combine the results of different surveys to make generalized and wide-sweeping conclusions.** For example, let's say your organization puts together a point-of-contact survey that is placed on public counters. You like the questions so much that you convert them to an online survey. Then you start mailing hard copies to customers as well.

Hold on! All of these ideas are great. In fact, that implementation plan meets our alignment strategy to a "T." The problem arises when you combine the results of all of those data sources into one big report. Do not commingle information from your various data-collection points!

The Science of Service

Think of each survey as a different piece of fruit. You have an apple (counter survey), an orange (web-based survey) and a pear (mail-out survey). The fact that they are all fruit ties them together. The fact that they all use the same survey questions also ties them together. So far, so good.

Now think about what you are trying to measure – the quality of the service delivery. You are looking over each piece of fruit, looking for blemishes, bruises, holes, discolorations, ripeness, etc. Each piece of fruit is very important and is judged solely based on how great it is compared to others of its kind. Pick up the apple. Smell it. Turn it over in your hand. Imagine the crunch! This is a darn fine apple. Now compare it to other fruits. You're looking for the same qualities in each piece of fruit but you are looking at them differently. If your apples feel like an orange, something is very wrong.

Stick with "apples to apples" comparisons. If you have a counter survey, compare it to other rounds of counter surveys. If you have a web survey, compare it to other web surveys. If you start mixing and commingling data, you'll end up with fruit salad. If you get a bad bite, how will you know which piece of fruit was responsible? How are you going to figure out how to fix it?

That being said, if you want to take an overall snapshot of a specific question (e.g. "Was the person you worked with knowledgeable?") across the entire organization and across survey types, that will tell you something. It will give you an overall picture. But remember, it's still fruit salad.

Let's take a closer look at the different types of surveys.

Face-to-Face Surveys

To get a "first impression" impact rating from an actual customer, conduct a survey at the moment that an in-person interaction has just been completed. Staff provides service and then BAM, the rating occurs. It's a point of contact, a snapshot in time, and is much more accurate than a recollection survey. (A recollection survey is completed sometime after the actual interaction. This could be a survey that is mailed out to a person who is asked to complete it and return it within a week or two.)

Why are they different, and why should you not commingle the data?

Think about it this way: I, the customer, just had an interaction with you and I'm really pleased. You were great! Big smile, good eye contact throughout the interaction followed by a "thank you for coming in today. Let me know if I can be of further assistance!" as we finish up. You made a great first impression, final impression and provided much help in between. I'm so pleased; I fill out a survey on the spot and rank every criterion a 5 out of 5. Excellent work!

Here's a second scenario: The same interaction occurs and I'm very happy with the service I received. Several days later, I receive a survey in the mail asking me to rate my experience. A lot has happened since then. I've made four dinners, cleaned the house, been stuck in traffic, got some bad news, had an argument with my neighbor and I'm not in the same mood I was in when you helped me four days ago. Now I fill out the survey. My recollection is that everything was just fine so I fill it out with all 3's and send it back. Or, more likely, I put it in the "to do" pile and don't fill it out at all.

If you have the opportunity to survey your client at the conclusion of the interaction, you will get different data (and likely more data) than if you send a survey later.

Mail-out Surveys

Mail-out surveys are most effective when you have an ongoing relationship with your customer. They work best with someone you see often enough to know who they are and feel connected to them in some way (dentist, landscaper, etc.).

There are several ways to increase the effectiveness of a mail-out survey. When you start a new survey, have staff introduce it to their clients. Give them copies of the new survey to show the clients before they leave the situation. Talk to them about the questions, and let the clients know it is important to you personally that they take the time to complete the survey and send it back.

Ask the client to agree to complete the survey. This creates a sense of importance or obligation. Once you have that agreement, you are much more likely to receive returned surveys than if you never mention it and the client later gets a survey in the mail without any connection to you, the service provider.

In "Magnetic Persuasion," Kurt Mortensen discusses the power of a sense of obligation in people, describing a study that sheds a lot of light on this. To paraphrase, the study observed a couple that went to the beach on two different days. They laid out their blanket, towels, radio, beach bag, chairs – everything a couple would need to enjoy a day at the beach. Then, they got up and went into the water. On both days, they paid a man to come by and try to steal their things.

On the first day, the couple simply got up, still talking to each other, and went into the water. When the paid "thief" came to steal their things, other beachgoers seemed to look the other way. In fact, only about 15 percent of the people tried to stop the thief.

On the second day, as the couple arrived and got situated, they made eye contact with people nearby and smiled at them. When they got up to go into the water, they asked their neighbors to watch their things while they enjoyed the water for a little while. Under these circumstances, 85 percent of the bystanders tried to stop the "thief." What a huge difference!

That's the power of obligation, and it will work with a survey, too, if you ask people to help.

Mystery Shopping

Mystery shopping is a method used to measure quality of service by using fake "customers" to pose as real customers performing routine tasks such as purchasing a product, asking questions, registering complaints or behaving in a certain way.

The stand-in reports to management about his or her experiences so that internal processes and procedures can be improved. Tools used in mystery shopping assessments range from simple questionnaires to audio and video recordings.

Mystery shopping helps us answer the important questions: do the skills your employees learned in class hold up in the real world? Are employees taking the culture of service efforts to heart?

They can and will if you tell them what success looks like (standards), give them the tools to achieve success (training) and hold them accountable (by gathering data).

A word to the wise: If you are going to launch a mystery shopping program, TELL EVERYONE! When organizations fail to notify employees before conducting such a program, it can easily be seen by staff as "spying" to catch people doing something wrong. This can be a disaster, quickly undermining all of your previous efforts to create a culture of service. After all, employees in a culture of service are respected and valued not spied on.

How to Design and Deploy a Successful Mystery Shopping Campaign

First, decide how much staff time to dedicate to this. There are a variety of ways to implement the program but be advised, it's a labor-intensive program to run, and the larger your organization, the more staff time will be needed.

When I worked with the County of San Diego, we took a three-pronged approach: we sent mystery shoppers in person, contacted staff over the phone and shopped public e-mail addresses posted on the website. There were only a few people in the Customer Service Center so we were able to do the e-mail shopping on our own but the in-person mystery shopping and phone shopping were assigned to a rotating team of 20 employee volunteers. The rotation of shoppers was critical. We couldn't physically conduct the shopping because we were so busy teaching classes and helping departments with the other essential elements that our faces had become well known.

First, create a master database of all public locations and public phone numbers where customers could visit or call for assistance. Then divide the list into sixths so one round could be conducted every other month (or whatever schedule works for you), and visit each location and call each phone number once per calendar year. (The County had 17,000 employees, and hudreds of phone numbers and office locations. Scale your efforts according to the size of your organization.) For in-person mystery shopping, the person would drive to a location, think of a question that a real customer would ask, go in and ask it then leave and rate the service.

I recommend in-person shopping be conducted using the basic persona of a regular average customer. This same persona should be used to send e-mails. On the phone, each call can be made three different ways: average caller, the problem customer and the wrong information customer.

A regular customer persona is someone who is in an average mood and asks one of your frequently asked questions (FAQs).

FAQs are critical to the success of any organization. A well-developed and maintained set of FAQs will:
- ▶ Ensure that all staff provide the same answers to common questions
- ▶ Provide consistency in service regardless of the employee's tenure
- ▶ Give customers the opportunity to self-serve
- ▶ Allow staff to spend precious hours on more complicated or unique situations rather than answering common questions multiple times throughout the day

Note on FAQs: There should be written FAQs prepared and maintained for each department or program that is being shopped. The FAQs should be updated annually; distributed to staff as part of regular staff meetings, new employee orientation and refresher trainings; and posted on the appropriate website.

A regular customer persona is used to measure the three prongs of great customer service: courtesy, knowledge and promptness. As discussed before, these three prongs should be covered under the formal list of standards and expectations, practiced in trainings and (according to Essential Element Four) measured to gather feedback.

A problem customer is someone who has a problem – or is a problem. This could be the customer who is not satisfied with the first answer. I highly recommend that this persona only be used over the phone not ever in person. (It's easy to see how problems can escalate and things could get ugly in person.)

Have employees from different departments shopping each other, and make sure that people who knew each other did not shop each other whether the shopping was in person, over the phone or via e-mail. We don't want any bad feelings interfering with relationships as it could be possible that staff members might later work together or attend the same meetings or trainings. We also don't want people favoring their friends or punishing those they don't like with overly good or bad ratings. That will give us skewed data.

"Problem" phone shoppers can be used to gauge employees' skills in working with difficult people or situations. Because customers of government are not always right, this can be a critical category. Government employees are often working with customers to enforce regulations and ensure legal guidelines are met. Working with the government, for example in permitting or code enforcement situations, can cost a customer time and money, and there are many situations where customers get angry and upset during the course of the interaction. Civil servants may also work with customers during crisis situations. It is extremely important the workers are well-versed in how to best handle difficult situations and people so they can control the situations as quickly and efficiently as possible without becoming part of the problem or internalizing too much stress in the course of duty.

Problem shoppers should be reserved only for phone assignments just like wrong information shoppers or wrong number shoppers. A wrong number shopper is exactly what it sounds like: a shopper calls a public phone number and when the employee answers, the shopper is surprised and says, "Oh, I'm sorry. I thought I was calling [another department]," or something to that effect. It's a good way to test the willingness of an employee to go out of his or her way to help the caller.

When I first started phone shopping about 10 years ago, I had a call that still stands out in my mind. I called an office and said, "I'm sorry, I thought I was calling the library. Do you have that number?"

The employee on the other end of the phone said, and I quote, "I'm not an operator, look it up yourself!" and hung up the phone.

How would the organization know this was occurring if we weren't mystery shopping by phone? How many other people did this employee treat that way before I called?

This type of interaction will become more and more rare while you are conducting your shopping program. In fact, as time goes on, you may find most of the obstacles to providing great service have nothing to do with the people. Processes are often the culprit.

For example, how are updates to your phone listings in the blue pages handled? Is there central coordination? Do the same people that fulfill the requests to change numbers notify the phone company to update the 4-1-1, 3-1-1 and other listings?

Another thing to take a look at is the way phone numbers are listed in your local directories. For example, some organizations list their phone numbers by department or program title. That's fine if you are looking for the director of a department but most customers have no idea what department or program they should call for their particular issue. (Heck, many employees of a government organization only know what their own program does.)

If our own employees don't know who to call when they need information, how can we expect our customers to know? For example, if you saw a deceased animal on the side of the road, who would you call to take care of it? Most people would probably call animal services or the sheriff's office. For one organization, the right answer is general services.

Create your phone listings and the provision of all of your information in a customer-first format. How would the customer look for that information? In this phone book scenario, one suggestion would be to list phone numbers by subject matter listings instead of department and program names.

One more tip for implementing a successful phone shopping program – understand your phone system. Are all of the numbers "on-net?" Meaning, do you have caller ID on the phones and can an employee tell if the call is coming from inside the agency or outside the agency? This is a huge "tell" for phone shopping. If all of your phones are networked, they can give your shoppers away. Here are two good options: have an "off-net" phone line installed or have staff use cell phones when mystery shopping by phone.

For an off-net phone, considerations include having it authorized by the powers that be and having all of your phone shoppers tethered to one location. On an off-net phone, schedule shopping appointments in a room with a door that closes.

Considerations for cell phones could include minutes used. If your organization issues work cell phones, do they all have the same area code and first three digits? If they do, could they be recognized as an internal call even though the caller is using a cell phone? If mystery shoppers use a personal cell phone, consider the minutes expended and possible costs incurred by the volunteer shopper.

Finally, let's address mystery shopping by e-mail. Most of the world communicates via e-mail now and here, more than in other form of interaction, we are seeing a generational clash.

While great service requires the same traits for everyone – nice, smart and fast – "everyone is a snowflake."

Not only do you have these various customers interpreting e-mails differently but you also have four generations and many, many backgrounds in the workplace, all guessing at the appropriate format and content of the e-mails that are sent on behalf of your organization.

Have you ever looked at your organization's outgoing e-mails? If not, do it NOW. Some people will amaze you with their professionalism; some e-mails will make your cringe or even shock and appall you.

Why are we leaving this huge arena of interaction to chance? Take the bull by the horns by applying the Six Essential Elements to e-mail communication.

▶ **EE1: Set e-mail expectations** – Include how quickly responses are expected and explain the desired content and format of the e-mails.

▶ **EE2: Tell your staff about the expectations** – Train people to be successful. Show them poorly written e-mails (with the sender's name removed, of course) and well-written e-mails.

▶ **EE3: Empower staff** – Make people part of upholding the great reputation of your organization. When you show staff the e-mails, ask them how it would make them feel if they were a customer on the receiving end. Ask about the impression they want to leave with their customers. Help them care.

▶ **EE4: Measure success** – This is where mystery shopping by e-mail comes in. It's the best way to get an objective measure on this major form of staff interaction with customers.

▶ **EE5: Rewards and Recognition** – Establish a recognition program for great e-mails. For example, the program or department with the highest rating gets acknowledged in the newsletter, an e-mail from the CEO or get some other form of acknowledgement. It doesn't have to cost anything to give people pride in their work and congratulate them for being the best at something.

▶ **EE6: Project/Process Improvement** – E-mail shopping may uncover opportunities for improvement that your organization has not yet considered.

- Are publicly posted e-mail addresses (the ones on your website) staffed by one individual or do several people have proxy for when a specific person is out of the office?
- Do all publicly posted e-mail addresses have an automatic response that customers receive immediately, thanking them for their messages and letting them know a staff person will be in touch within 48 hours?
- Do all e-mail addresses in the organization follow the same format (i.e. wbrick@ or wendi.brick@ or wendib@ etc.)?
- Do all of e-mail addresses have the same URL?

As you move forward with the e-mail mystery shopping to measure your success, here are a few tips to keep in mind.

▶ Establish anonymous e-mail addresses to send your inquiry e-mails from. You can use Hotmail, Google or Yahoo as examples for new (free) e-mail accounts.

▶ Change the e-mail accounts each time you conduct a new round of mystery shopping. Especially in smaller organizations (a few hundred people or less), it's hard to stay anonymous. Once employees know there is mystery shopping including e-mail shopping, they quickly start guessing which accounts are the shoppers' accounts.

As soon as you start a mystery shopping campaign, staff will assume that a ton of their interactions are with mystery shoppers. In the vast majority of situations, it won't be true. Employees always assume that the program is much more widespread than it is. This is an amazing phenomenon, one that will go far to promote the great service you are championing. In the end, it only matters that anyone could be a shopper. If the program keeps people on their toes, it is supporting a culture of outstanding service for every person, every day.

Remember: Communicate honestly about the mystery shopping program before it is deployed. Tell everyone you can exactly what the program is about and eliminate all the "catch me messing up, Big Brother, no trust, no value, looking to punish us" thoughts that go through employees' minds. Helping people understand the program and succeed when they are "shopped."

As soon as you start a mystery shopping campaign, staff will assume that a ton of their interactions are with mystery shoppers.

Communicate: Several months before you implement the program, develop a communications plan. Discuss it at staff meetings, post information on your intranet site, send an organization-wide e-mail, hold open meetings and forums, go to the employee groups and labor organizations, and reach out in other ways. This is what to communicate.

- ▶ Why this program is being implemented
- ▶ When and how often the "shopping" will happen
- ▶ Whether it will be in person, on the phone and/or via e-mail
- ▶ The criteria on which employee interactions will be rated
  - Yes, give your team the ratings forms
  - We want them to be great at this all the time – so tell them exactly what it takes to be great
- ▶ How the data will be tabulated and reported
- ▶ Which people, phone numbers and/or e-mails will be shopped
- ▶ How everyone in the organization and the customers will benefit from this new program

If you take these communications seriously and apply the Six Essential Elements to each type of shopping, your organization will see tremendous improvements in service delivery very quickly (and you will not be seen as a "spy for the suits downtown").

Setting the Stage – and Rating the Performances

Following are two additional ways to measure success; both are extremely effective and they tie-in perfectly with everything we've covered about creating a culture of service.

First, include "Provides outstanding customer service to every person, every day" as a line item on your employee performance reviews. This positions you to be proactive instead of reactive.

And second, use a 360-degree review. Also known as multi-source feedback, a "360" provides feedback from all around an employee. (The "360" refers to the 360 degrees in a circle, with an individual figuratively in the center of the circle.) Feedback is provided by subordinates, peers and supervisors, and also includes a self-assessment. In some cases, feedback from external sources such as customers and suppliers is solicited as well. Results are often used to plan training and development, make administrative decisions or for internal evaluation. (There is a fair amount of controversy as to whether 360-degree reviews should be used exclusively for development purposes or for appraisal purposes as well.)

One reason 360s are so powerful is because people are on their best behavior around the boss but they often show their typical behaviors to the internal and external customers around them. The way people treat those they don't "have" to be nice to is a true measure of a culture of service.

In my career, I rose up through seven levels in various organizations starting as a student worker and leaving as a department director. I ran in the same circles for all those years, and although people certainly moved around, I often ran into the same people over and over again. Low-ranking people moved

The Science of Service

up, sometimes ahead of their supervisors. And they remembered exactly how they were treated when their title wasn't so impressive.

If you really want to know if staff members are treating everyone well and truly support a culture of service, conduct anonymous 360s. If you really want to know if you are doing all you can to empower staff (Essential Element Four) – ask them about their supervisors. The 360s provide great insight and very focused coaching for everyone in your organization.

If you have organizational development staff in-house, they may be able to design a 360 for everyone to use. If not, there are many tools to be found online.

For all the reasons you believe that great service is absolutely vital to your organization, and to each and every one of the employees, you must have a way to measure the quality of your supervisors. If front-line employees are the face of the organization, supervisors are the backbone. If the supervisors are not supporting your efforts through their own actions, your culture of service cannot withstand.

All that said, do the 360s.

Chapter Seven

Essential Element Five: Celebrate Success with Employee Recognition Programs

Rewards and recognition programs can – and should – come in many colors and flavors. There are a lot of different ways to tell people they are doing a great job. You can praise them as individuals and as groups. Reward them publicly or privately. They can be recognized for a job well done during a specific time or situation.

Regardless of how you reward your employees, all reward programs should have several things in common.

First and foremost, the criteria for acknowledgement should be tied directly to the behavior(s) that you want to enforce. This book is all about customer service so guess what criteria we're focusing on? The three core components of great service: promptness, courtesy and knowledge.

Second, rewards and recognition should be fun. This is an opportunity to celebrate – and celebration at work is critical. I have always been a strong advocate for celebrating great successes and great failures. Part of growing and maturing and getting better at what you do is failing. If you are going to fail, fail big, get it over with and move on. Here's an example of this principle in action.

Years ago, I hired student interns for the summer; they were just out of high school. We trained one of them (for this example we'll call her Debbie) to take calls on a public hotline. Sometimes the callers were upset so Debbie needed a lot of coaching to work through difficult situations.

One day I looked up and she was standing in my office doorway. She didn't say a word. I asked Debbie what was up and she started crying. "I did my best but this man on the phone was so upset and he just kept yelling at me! I kept trying but then he hung up on me!" She felt terrible, thinking she had let down the team and worrying that he would call back and complain about her service. She didn't want to get in trouble.

I smiled sympathetically and told her, "This happens sometimes even when we try our best. We'll work on it some more together." Then I suggested we debrief with the team.

I walked Debbie into the main room and asked everyone to join me in a standing ovation for our young intern. "She has just been initiated by her first really difficult caller thereby formally joining the ranks of our hotline group. Let's give her a round of applause!"

The group really came through, cheering, whistling, smiling, standing and clapping. Our young intern starting smiling then laughing. It really made her feel like part of the team.

Then I asked her, when she was ready, to come back to my office to go through the call with me so we could continue to help her mature as a call center staff member and she would be more successful next time.

That's probably not the kind of story you were expecting to hear in a rewards and recognition chapter. But this was a young, impressionable person with no experience. By doing what we did, we used this "failure" to learn and build her self-confidence. As a team, we backed her up on a rough day, and that changed everything for her. We showed her that we understood, that we've all experienced difficult calls and that she shouldn't take it personally. And we set her up to look at this situation in a positive way so she would continue to improve her skills.

The Science of Service

Had we not seized this opportunity to celebrate, we could have lost her - mentally and physically. If she held onto that negative experience, she would have shut down and started avoiding the phones or the team (because she wouldn't feel as good as them). Following a traumatic situation like this, some people begin calling in sick or worse not showing up at all! As a student, she could have just quit which would have left us short-handed for the rest of the summer. Those few minutes of celebration benefited us all in a big way.

Spontaneous moments of celebration and recognition are powerful but they should not take the place of traditional rewards and recognition programs. These should be formalized, and the criteria for awards communicated in advance.

Rewarding people shows people they are valued. Notice, I didn't say "makes them feel like they are valued." There's nothing persuasive or phony about a great recognition program. If your goal is to set up a shell program for the sole purpose of pretending that your staff are important, just put the book down and walk away. It won't work. If you genuinely believe that your team matters – that this organization is nothing without the dedicated work of talented and creative individuals, that every single person, regardless of title, is just as important as everyone else – then please read on.

In government in general, and especially in these economically-challenging times, we must focus on extremely low- or no-cost ways to reward and recognize our team. That's perfectly fine! What is unacceptable is saying that we can't afford to recognize great work. It's just not true. The reality is that people are not strongly motivated by money. People are motivated by their innate need to be valued as part of a team.

Here are some great ideas that cost nothing or almost nothing to implement.

▶ A hand-written thank you card
▶ A quick text message to someone's cell phone
▶ A printed letter from the department director, chief administrator or elected official
▶ A brag wall where people can post positive comments and thank you notes
▶ Recognition at staff meetings
▶ Employee-to-employee awards
▶ Department-to-department recognition ("We couldn't have done it without you!")
▶ Kudos in newsletters or spotlights on the website
▶ Employee of the day or month

Regardless of how you choose to recognize your teammates, do something. Tie the recognition back to the standards and expectations you've already established for great customer service. That way, you are reinforcing the behaviors you would like to repeat.

Remember that recognition programs get old and need to be refreshed. Once an award becomes common, it loses value. Be sure to change up your reward programs periodically.

A Vision of "Care-ful" Service

Use the power of rewards, recognition and celebration to support the culture you want to create. This ties the vision to action.

The importance of a great customer service vision and strong associated values really should not be underestimated. The vision and values of the team help individuals make quick decisions and take focused action in any situation. If a team has a vision, keeps a good sense of humor and treats the internal customers as well as the external customers, the right choices in each situation become obvious.

For example, Southwest Airlines posted its vision on its website: "Southwest Cares." That's all it says – and that's all that needs to be said. Two words align the entire company – and they could apply to any company or organization.

In every decision, internal or external, how do we show that we care? Which choices show that we care? What tone of voice shows we care? How do we care for each other and our customers every day?

What if you were part of a government call center in charge of issuing food stamps? For those who have been case workers or worked in a government call center, you know how difficult this job is and how challenging the customer interactions can be. What if the call center's customer service vision was, "We care"? Could that change the way you and your team addressed your customers' needs – and how they felt about your organization in return? *Absolutely.*

Champion your vision with rewards and recognition, and your team will thank you in more ways than one.

The Science of Service

Chapter Eight

Essential Element Six:
Projects and Process Improvement

During the course of implementing the first Five Elements, especially Element Four (feedback), certain things will come to light – processes that aren't working properly and projects that, if completed, would vastly improve service delivery.

If a genuine, sustainable culture of service is to exist and evolve, we must address the concept of:

- ► Procedures
- ► People
- ► Processes
- ► And Technology

3P+T™

In Chapter 3 (Setting Expectations), we addressed procedures by making sure the expectations of staff were written down and specific, setting employees up to succeed and embracing the organization's vision of great service. Most people really do want to do a good job, and if they know what defines "a good job," the majority of people will likely keep those expectations in mind.

People are the core of every organization. Without the people, there is no organization. A strong culture of service always helps employees develop the skills they need to meet expectations and supports them in their efforts by reinforcing how integral each and every employee is in meeting the vision and making the program successful.

In 12 years of conducting customer satisfaction surveys, I've seen some interesting trends. When a survey is initially deployed, it is likely that some opportunities for improvement (involving both people and procedures) will be discovered. These are generally fixed relatively quickly. For example, low ratings in courtesy and knowledge can be addressed quickly.

The real challenge comes with systemic issues, the big process type issues that show up over and over and over again. These are harder to get a handle on and may involve an investment of funds which requires advance planning.

One common systemic issue is promptness. Government offices are notorious for being slow and having long, complicated, cumbersome processes that seem to take forever. This issue tends to show up again and again, earning the lowest ratings on government customer service surveys.

This really is not surprising especially to those who work in the public sector. Think about this from a historical perspective. Many of our organizations have been in existence, doing the work of the people for 100 years or more. How much has changed during that time in culture, technology, attitudes, legislation, regulations and society in general? It's not easy for a government agency with limited funding to keep up.

Think about the numbers. Every time you started a new job, didn't you try to change things a little to make them better? Well, how many people, with all their various job titles and iterations (we like to reorganize in government) have had that job or its predecessor jobs before you? How many years of changes, piled on years of changes, have there been? Is it really any surprise that, after 100 years in operation and 15-20 different people leading the program, processes get complicated and end up taking too long?

Some of these processes may come quickly to mind. We all have steps that make us want to roll our eyes every time we have to do them. We ask ourselves, "Why on earth does this have to take so long?!" Or we avoid doing certain types of projects because we ourselves are daunted by the red tape!

Why would our organization want us to waste time on processes that are antiquated, lengthy and, let's be honest, semi-pointless in some cases? Looking at process and project improvements speaks directly to making our workdays more efficient and cutting out all of the wasted steps that add no value but destroy our promptness.

Because our processes have evolved over such a long period of time and because there have been so many cooks in the kitchen, government processes are absolutely loaded with "low-hanging fruit," meaning very obvious ways to quickly improve efficiency. One way to identify these opportunities is to conduct a "Red Rules/Blue Rules" workshop (see below).

And what about procedures? We've already discussed our organizations' propensity for tribal knowledge and learning rather than producing written guidelines. If we focus on our people as our first customers, streamlining processes and writing out procedures for standardization and consistency, we would make great strides in providing amazing service—both internally and externally.

Then there is technology. Big. Expensive. Technology.

Many organizations are upgrading and embracing technology. A word to the wise: make sure your business processes are driving technology and not the other way around. Technology is not a universal solution to improving efficiency. When a bad process without standards and procedures is automated, it becomes a bad automated process.

Red Rules/Blue Rules Exercise:

Gather a group of people who represent a cross-section of employees in your particular program area. Be sure to include:

- ▶ Supervisors
- ▶ Front-line staff
- ▶ Field staff
- ▶ Managers
- ▶ Tenured employees
- ▶ New employees
- ▶ Older employees
- ▶ Younger employees

Ask them to **question everything they do in their workday**. After you've blown their minds by giving them permission to do this, the real fun begins.

Ask them to sort their observations into two categories. Red rules are processes you follow because you have a legal mandate to do so. This might include federal air-quality mandates, stringently managed programs, etc.

Blue rules include all the internal policies and procedures such as needing five copies of something for filing or the protocol for travel expense reimbursement or the procedure to report to elected officials. Hint: You know a process is a blue rule when you ask, "Why do we do it this way?" and the answer is, "Because it's always been done that way."

Arrange people to get a good cross-section of demographics at each table; it's really interesting to see their various perspectives on the rules. Have them make a list of challenges to every red rule and blue rule. Ask them to recommend updates, changes or whether the rule should be discontinued.

Challenge them to think through the results. Why does the rule exist? Is it still required? What rules or policies should be rewritten? Do we need new ones?

This type of workgroup can have spectacular consequences. Beyond creating a lot of ideas to improve processes, these interactions:

- ▶ Involve and recognize the employees as experts in their jobs
- ▶ Bring all levels of employees into the decision-making process
- ▶ Establish synergy and bring opinions and thoughts together in a new way
- ▶ Uncover nuances that would not be discussed during a regular workday
- ▶ Bring staff closer together to strengthen the team environment

These benefits extend throughout the organization in part because people really appreciate the opportunity to help reshape the wheel – not just be a cog in one that's already rolling along.

Improvement Projects and the IT Connection

In the ongoing effort to streamline and update the organization, certain improvement projects will inevitably arise. Many, if not all, of these projects are inextricably linked and dependent on the organization's information technology capabilities.

Therefore, I strongly advise you to become good friends with your IT person. Many customer service improvement projects cannot happen without this type of support. Direct access and smooth relations with this department will inevitably add speed and efficiency to your initiatives.

Automation is one of the best ways to make things easier, faster and more efficient for your customers.

When it comes to customer service process improvement, your IT person should be like your right hand. Think about it. With all the interfaces your customers have with your organization, automation is one of the best ways to make things easier, faster and more efficient for your customers.

Examples that come up again and again include new phone systems and contact centers. The contact center is the heartbeat of your organization whether it's a basic call center of 5-10 people or a 3-1-1 call center with 100 team members. Reliable, updated technology facilitates smooth call distribution and supports a robust call quality monitoring program. It also allows you to build work flow processes, customer relationship management systems, knowledge base databases and scripted responses to frequently asked questions.

While the technology will *allow* you to provide these things, it's the customer service people who affect the quality of the content. These employees are the ones who work to make sure that the scripting has the proper tone, content and impact. When the technology and employees are in sync, it sets the staff up to be courteous, knowledgeable and prompt. The IT people make that possible.

Remember to streamline all processes *before* they are automated to ensure the process will be as efficient and effective as possible. This is a very common mistake in a lot of organizations.

Before you automate anything, first conduct a streamlining event. There are many different methods; I prefer a Kaizen-driven event.

Using Kaizen in Government

Kaizen, directly translated from Japanese, means "change for the better." It refers to a philosophy or practices that focus upon continuous improvement of processes and involves all employees from the CEO to the new hire. By improving standardized processes, Kaizen aims to eliminate waste, repetition and inefficiency. Successful implementation requires the participation of the workers.

First implemented in several Japanese businesses after World War II, it was embraced by Toyota at a time when Toyotas were seen as something of a junk car – disposable. That reputation, as well as the product line, was completely transformed with Kaizen. The Kaizen process works quickly and produces astounding results – even in government where the processes are not as visible as they are in manufacturing. At the core of a Kaizen event is to "make visible" those things which are not visible. It uses process mapping techniques to reveal all the steps of a process.

When you have a business process, you can't see it so it's hard to streamline. You can go out into an office space and you can see that everyone is working. They are on the phone or on the computer. They are reading papers or writing notes. They are in conference with a group or meeting with individuals. Sure, everyone is busy. But what are they really doing? Where are they in the process in relation to the beginning and end? Are they even working on steps that are necessary and add value or are they getting stuck in non-essential steps that waste time and are really not necessary? We have absolutely no way of knowing until we map it out.

Another aspect of Kaizen that makes it so effective is that it brings together all of the experts. A Kaizen event is generally several days long with all of the players and decision-makers engaged and present in the room at the same time. Therefore, at the conclusion of the event, real solutions have been realized by everyone and can be implemented quickly.

Because all affected parties are in the room (including representatives from other departments or organizations), every person at every touch point has ownership of and buy-in to the new process. No one is left out and no one feels "put-upon" and resistant.

Having all the decision-makers in one room is a huge plus, too. If there were staff members only, they would very likely come up with a new process or plan that, once presented to the decision-makers, could be denied due to extenuating circumstances that the staff were not aware of. With everyone in one room, all discrepancies and ideas can be hashed out then and there so people walk away with an action plan and a "to do" list. Once that list is implemented, the new processes are established.

A truly amazing and telling moment comes when 10 or so people are sitting in a room, mapping out a process, and are suddenly stunned to realize just how many steps are involved! Many people involved only see their own piece. They are aware of the fact that there are others involved but they almost never realize the extent of others' roles or the impact they have on the people in the other departments or agencies.

More "a-ha" moments come when you have two or three people who follow the same process every day and then they realize that they really don't follow the same process at all! There is incredible variability from person to person in government organizations even when they think they are doing the same thing. When they map out the process – step 1 leads to step 2 which leads to step 3 – they start disagreeing.

Variability is a huge problem in implementing government processes. Every person implementing the process may be doing it differently. Variability is exacerbated by the fact that many procedures are not written down; decisions can fall into gray areas and are subject to interpretation.

At the base level, efficiency = no variability. Quality control aims to eliminate variability. Set the quality and efficiency bars where you want them then engineer a system so that every single person implements that process the same no matter who they are or what personality type they have.

Michael E. Gerber wrote one of my favorite books - *The E-Myth*. It uses the success of McDonald's as an example of limiting variability in operations. It's written from a business point of view but the concepts are certainly applicable to public-sector processes as well.

Kaizen-driven events are exhausting, exhilarating and tremendously satisfying for the participants as well as the facilitator. They fly in the face of the standard practice of forming a committee to solve a problem and meeting for two hours every month for a year – which is a great method for ongoing improvement but not as effective in fixing something that's broken.

Using the committee process to fix a process is, in and of itself, inefficient! Why not get the committee, as the subject matter experts they are, in a room together for three or four days? It's the same investment of time in the end but the results are far superior. Not only do you get results but you also get a committed group of people who have bonded around a shared and emotional experience, and they become die-hard champions for the cause going forward.

Moving back a few steps, remember the section about involving your IT people in process improvements? Your IT should be in the room during the Kaizen event, too. There will be many ideas for automation tossed around, and someone technical should be there to say if the ideas are possible or practical, and what it would take to implement them.

If any of your critical team members are not present during the Kaizen event, you are setting yourself up for a disaster. First of all, one missing person can blow up all the work that you did. Do you want to commit 15 key people in your department and stakeholders groups to a four-day event, only to find out afterwards that everything they came up with isn't going to work? Talk about an epic failure!

A side note: A Kaizen event is an exhausting and emotionally-draining experience. It's meant to be. It pushes people to creatively solve a problem that they haven't been able to solve before. There are arguments. There is depression. There is anxiety. Facilitating a Kaizen event is not for the inexperienced or the faint of heart. The facilitator becomes almost a spiritual leader, helping people go through the process productively and come out the other end with a great solution.

The real breakthroughs come after the group peaks and troughs and then levels out. The group will not create the team bond and establish the energy that people need to sustain the implementation after the event if they don't stick together and stay focused on their common cause.

At the conclusion of the event, the team creates an action plan and commits to making its piece happen. There may also be a presentation to other interested parties that will be affected by the process after it is changed.

In addition to the Kaizen event itself, there are two additional critical components for success.

The pre-event scoping meeting. A skilled Kaizen facilitator sits down with the leaders of the process improvement project, those few people who have the assignment to improve the process. They know the "who, what, when, where and why" of the project. The facilitator will have them walk through the process as they know it from start to finish.

This process overview is critical because it gives the facilitator an idea of how long each step in the Kaizen event will take. For example, some processes such as a discretionary permitting process are wildly complicated and could take several years from start to finish. Some processes are internal to one department and may take several months from start to finish. This is critical information for scheduling purposes. It would be disastrous to run out of time during an event before finishing the process.

The facilitator also uses the pre-scoping meeting to figure out who should be in the room. Who knows this process backward and forward? Who are the people in other departments/agencies that work with this process? Are there external stakeholders who could be involved? Which IT person will be in the room, and the manager/decision-maker? And who is the wild card? (This is an unrelated person who is smart and insightful and creative, and has a great reputation for being an upbeat problem-solver. This person provides a fresh perspective, suggests solutions that people who are close to the process may not think of and questions or challenges the group in a positive way.)

The pre-scoping meeting usually occurs about 30 days before the event itself. This gives the lead time to make the logistical arrangements, invite guests, schedule a room, arrange for catering, etc. Yes, arrange for catering. Stop laughing! Seriously. If you have an event that runs for several consecutive days, you are holding people captive in the room. It is important that they be present for the entire event. No cell phones. No BlackBerries. Everyone takes breaks together. This requires catering. And lots of coffee.

Post-Event Meeting: The third and final piece of a Kaizen event is the post-event meeting. This meeting brings together the project lead and some of the more involved subject matter experts. The discussion centers on what has gone well in the initial stages of implementing the action plan and what obstacles they encountered that they didn't foresee. The facilitator helps the group work through some obstacles so the project will stay on-track.

Does this sound exhausting and like a huge commitment of staff time and effort? Good, because it is. And it's still the absolute best way to quickly streamline processes and generate tremendous results. Kaizen events have been known to reduce existing processes by 75 percent. Isn't it worth it?

Chapter Nine
Tying It All Together

Here are a few extra/wrap-up tips to support your efforts to develop a culture of service in your organization.

Tip #1: If you are just starting on this process, start with a gap analysis. What are you doing now in each of the Six Essential Elements? What could you be doing? Ideally, you would compare your activities to best practices to identify the gaps. Once you have those gaps identified, you are well on your way to putting together an action plan.

Tip #2: Put someone in charge of making it happen. Who's going to implement your customer service initiatives? Choose someone who has a great attitude and service predisposition, is willing to learn and loves to talk. A lot.

Tip #3: The way you behave will strongly influence the way your staff behaves. Actions speak louder than words. The way you treat your people, and the way your people see you treat others, will seriously affect their behavior. Remember, the leader sets the tone. It's your commitment to raise the bar that your people are feeding off of.

In Conclusion

If you only supervise two people, you can implement the Six Essential Elements. If you run an entire organization, you can implement the Six Essential Elements. Whatever positive action steps you take will move you closer to the end game – a superior customer service philosophy and vision. YOU set it up to succeed.

And that's how we all succeed: we start with a vision, develop a methodology and design an action plan to fill the gaps over time.

Please try to apply this material. Great service in government is not an oxymoron. You have the power as an individual to make a difference. You can maximize your customers' experience and be part of improving your organizations reputation in the community, one person at a time.

Go do great things.

About

Wendi Pomerance Brick

In 1998, Wendi became the County of San Diego's first Customer Service Manager. She was responsible for developing the nationally-recognized Customer Service Center which has been used as a model for other government organizations around the United States. This program included an aggressive training program during which thousands of the 17,000 person workforce were trained.

The Customer Service Center was awarded two NACo (National Association of Counties) Achievement Awards, and in 2003, Wendi was a finalist in the *San Diego Business Journal*'s annual "Women Who Mean Business."

It was in 2003 that Wendi formed Customer Service Advantage, Inc. to provide customer service improvement training and consultation to other organizations. With her expertise in customer service in government, working with a diverse workforce and working within unionized environments driven by rules and regulations, Wendi's unique approach to training and creating a customer-focused culture was in demand.

In November 2006, Wendi became the City of San Diego's Director of the Department of Customer Services. The department was responsible for many programs in this organization of 10,000 including citywide training and developing and deploying customer satisfaction surveys.

CSA, Inc. has been in operation since 2003, and incorporated in 2009. Wendi now focuses her efforts as the full-time President and Chief Executive Officer.

The Mission of CSA, Inc. is to "Maximize the experience of our customers' customers." CSA, Inc. tailors its approach to customer service for government organizations, educational institutions, non-profit organizations and private businesses. CSA, Inc. offers customer service training, process improvement workshops, customer satisfaction survey development and customer service best practices gap analyses.

The Science of Service
Six Essential Elements for
Creating a Culture of Service
In the Public Sector

Yes, I want to implement the Six Essential Elements in my sphere of influence!

Please have a representative contact me. I would like to:
- ▶ know more about how CSA, Inc. could help me implement the ideas you discuss in "The Science of Service", and/or
- ▶ arrange for a speaker on these topics at an upcoming event.

Name:_____

Organization: _____

Address: _____

City/State/ZIP: _____

E-mail address: _____

✔ Please sign me up to receive the monthly free ENewsletter from CSA, Inc. – "The CSA Edge"

Daytime phone number:_____

Number of employees: _____

Number of locations: _____

Your role in the organization:_____

Four ways to contact us:
Visit our website: www.theCSAedge.com, Call CSA, Inc.: 760.445.6550,
E-mail: info@theCSAedge.com, or write at:

Customer Service Advantage, Inc
555 Country Club Lane, Suite C-350
Escondido, CA 92026